Handcrafted designs & techniques

POLYMER CLAY

JEWELRY WORKSHOP

Sian Hamilton

First published 2015 by
Guild of Master Craftsman Publications Ltd
Castle Place, 166 High Street, Lewes,
East Sussex BN7 1XU

Text © GMC Publications, 2015
Copyright in the Work © GMC Publications Ltd, 2015

Step photography by the jewelry designers; all other
photography by Laurel Guilfoyle.

Each contributor has been acknowledeged alongside
their project.

ISBN 978 1 78494 045 4

A catalog record for this book is available from the
British Library.

Publisher Jonathan Bailey
Production Manager Jim Bulley
Senior Project Editor Dominique Page
Editor Sarah Doughty
Managing Art Editor Gilda Pacitti
Art Editor Luana Gobbo

Set in ITC Century BT

Color origination by GMC Reprographics

Printed and bound in China

POLYMER CLAY
JEWELRY WORKSHOP

Contents

INTRODUCTION

Polymer clay is one of the most versatile mediums available for jewelry making. You can mix pretty much any color and with the addition of pearl, translucent, and metallic colors the world of polymer is your oyster! It's affordable and can be baked in a standard oven so you don't need lots of specialist equipment either. This book takes you on a journey through the diverse styles achievable with polymer clay. Don't worry if you haven't tried it before—it's really easy to use.

I am Sian Hamilton and I have been making jewelry for over 30 years. From the plastic string of beads I made as a child and wore with pride through to a BA (honours) degree in 3D design specializing in jewelry, I have been immersed in design my entire life. These days I make and sell jewelry by commission, have recently written a couple of books about jewelry making and am also the Editor of a magazine for jewelry makers called *Making Jewellery*. The magazine has many amazingly talented designers creating beautiful projects. It is these designers that created the stunning projects in this book.

Color is a very personal thing, and if the ones used in projects throughout this book don't appeal to you then swap to the color palette of your choice. As long as you stick with the same brand of clay (don't mix different brands in the same piece, because they have different baking temperatures) then you can use any colors you like. Above all, have fun—polymer clay is great to use with kids, so you can get the whole family involved, too.

Tools & Equipment

To make the projects in this book you will need the following tools and equipment.

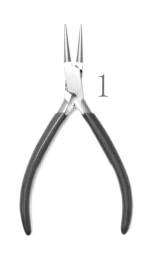

1 Pliers

There are many types of pliers available that do different jobs. The ones that are used most when starting out are round-nose (pictured), flat-nose, and chain-nose pliers.

2 Side cutters

Used for cutting excess wire, a pair of side cutters is essential when putting jewelry pieces together.

3 Pasta machine

Of all the tools you can use with polymer clay a pasta machine is the most useful. It helps you to roll out sheets of clay to an even thickness in a matter of seconds and also conditions the clay very easily. All pasta machines have different numerical settings; here is a quick guide to follow.
Thickest setting: No.1 – approx. ⅛in (3mm), 10 playing cards
Medium setting: No.2 or No.3 – approx. ¹⁄₁₆in (1.5–2mm), 7–8 playing cards
Thin setting: No.4 or No.5 – approx. ¹⁄₃₂in (0.75–1mm), 4–5 playing cards

4 Tissue blade

These blades are razor sharp on one long edge. It's a good idea to identify and mark this sharp edge for yourself with a permanent marker pen. Blades come in various lengths and also with a ripple (wavy) effect. If you don't have a tissue blad, a craft knife will do.

5 Work surface

You will need a flat work surface for the projects. Tiles work well, as the polymer pieces can be baked straight on the tile. There are also flexible, non-stick surfaces available, such as Teflon.

6 Shape cutters

Made from metal or plastic, these cutters come in a wide variety of shapes and can be purchased from sugarcraft suppliers as well as craft stores.

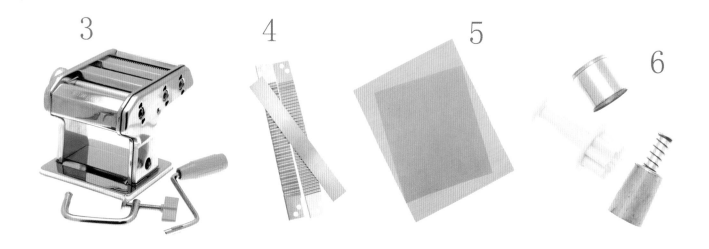
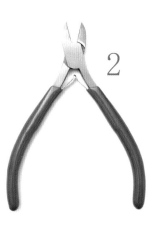

7 Needle tool

Used for poking holes in clay and cutting around shapes, this tool has a sharp pointed end, so use carefully.

8 Pin vise and drill bits

The pin vise is a handheld tool for drilling holes into polymer clay using drill bits.

9 Extruder

This tool comes with discs with different shapes cut out. The clay is fed in the tube and you twist the handle to extrude the clay through the disc, which forms a long snake in the shape of the cutters in the discs.

10 Roller and spacers

Any long, straight rod can be used as a rolling pin or you can use a craft roller. Spacers are plastic bars with a set depth, so you can achieve an evenly rolled sheet of clay by placing them either side of the clay before rolling.

11 Texture makers

Texture mats have patterns inlayed into them that transfer onto polymer clay. You can use anything to make a texture on clay, such as sponges, fabric, or lace.

12 Silk screens

These are like mini versions of silk screens for fabric. You lay the screen on top of the clay sheet and push acrylic paint over the screen, transferring the design onto the clay.

13 Bead pins

These are long steel pins with a pointed end for making holes in beads; the beads can be baked on the pins to help hold the shape.

14 Sandpaper

Wet and dry sandpapers are good for polymer clay, using the fine grits like 400 and 800. If you want a really high shine finish then use micromesh in grades 1800 and 3200. The higher the number on these papers the finer the grit.

7

8

9

10

11

12

13

14

Modeling Materials

Alongside polymer clay, there are a few other modeling materials you will need—all readily available and relatively inexpensive to buy.

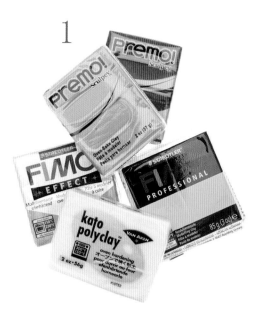

1

1 Polymer clay

There are many brands of polymer clay available and some of the projects mention brands such as Premo! Sculpey® and Fimo, so you can get the exact colors for the piece that is shown. If making the piece in another color then any brand of clay can be used. All brands have different baking temperatures and they can all be baked in a standard oven. Always refer to the manufacturer's recommended temperature. Do not bake any hotter or you may burn the clay.

2 Liquid polymer clay

There are a number of different brands of liquid polymer clay that bake clear but all work slightly differently. In general, they are used for sticking together baked clay, image transfer, and as a glaze. They can be tinted to make colors as well. Refer to the brand for baking instructions.

3 Silicone cream clay and Deco sauce

Like silicone you use for home repairs, this product looks like whipped cream, while Deco sauce resembles fruit syrup. They are used mostly for projects making miniature food in conjunction with miniature crockery.

4 Miniature cane

These come already baked and made into tiny things like fruit slices for use with miniature food projects.

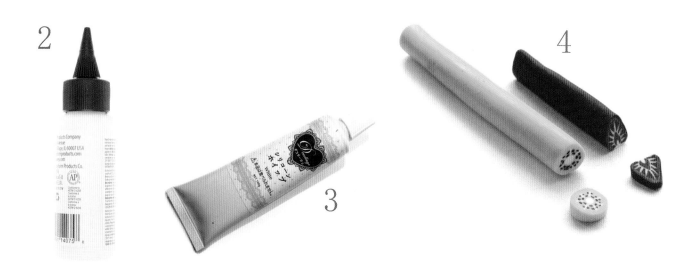

2

3

4

5 Gilder's paste, acrylic paint, or oil paint

These are all types of products that are used to color the surface of polymer clay. Different brands work on baked and unbaked clay.

6 Varnish

Water-based varnish is great for polymer clay but do not use solvent-based products. Many clay brands sell varnish to go with their products.

7 Alcohol inks

Alcohol inks are an intensely concentrated dye dissolved in alcohol. They are used to color pale or translucent clay.

8 Metal foil

These are wafer-thin sheets of foil that can be added to the surface of the clay to give a metallic finish. Always use metal foils that have been developed for use with polymer clay.

9 Metallic powder

Fine powders with a metallic shine can be used to coat either baked or unbaked clay. They can be mixed into clay or rubbed on the surface.

10 Metallic pen

There are many brands of metallic pen that can be used on baked clay. Don't use on unbaked clay.

11 Polyester batting

This is the thick fiber fabric that dressmakers use for filling. It is used with polymer clay to stop the clay from getting a flat point when being baked on a tray, as the batting supports the clay.

12 Adhesive

There are lots of glues that work with polymer clay as long as the clay has been baked. Cyanoacrylate adhesives (superglue) and two-part epoxy resins work well. Thick gel glues are good for sticking findings such as brooch bars to baked polymer, as they create a very firm hold.

Jewelry Materials

Listed below are the stringing materials and findings you will need in order to turn your polymer clay pieces into jewelry.

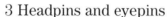

1 Clasps
There are many different types of clasp available, including slides, bolts, triggers, and even magnetic varieties. Choose a clasp to suit your design.

2 Jumprings
A jumpring is a single ring of wire that is used to join pieces together. They come in every size you can think of and many different colors.

3 Headpins and eyepins
These are pieces of wire with a flat or ball end (headpin) or a loop at the end (eyepin). Thread a bead on the wire and make a loop at the open end to secure the bead in place. Eyepins can be linked together to make a chain.

4 Earwires
Earwires come in various styles, from a simple "U"-shape with a loop, to ones with a bead and coil finish. The loop is opened to thread on the earring piece.

5 Cord ends
These are used to secure cord. Necklace or cord ends have side flaps that fold over the cord.

6 Crimp beads and covers
Crimp beads look like small metal beads with large holes or tubes. They work by compressing stringing materials together to hold them in place. Used with crimp beads, crimp covers go over the crimp to make it look like a normal small bead.

7 Calottes
Calottes are hinged cups, used to attach a jewelry design to a clasp. They give a much better finish than simply tying a knot around a jumpring or clasp.

8 Bails
A bail is a finding that you use to attach a pendant piece to a necklace. They are mostly made of metal and have a space for the necklace cord and a loop at the bottom for a jumpring where the pendant is attached.

9 Nylon-coated wire
This wire is really good for stringing, as it has a better strength for heavy beads than ordinary threads. It also holds a nice shape on the neck.

10 Leather, cord, and suede
These types of cords come in various colors and thicknesses. They can be knotted securely with ease or used with ribbon crimps or neck ends.

11 Wire
Wire comes in a large range of sizes. When starting out, buy plated wire, as it is much cheaper than precious metal. Look for a non-tarnishing variety so it doesn't discolor against your skin.

12 Chain
There are many styles of chain and a variety of colors available. Fine chains are good for hanging pendants and large link chains are good for making charm bracelets or when adding beads to the individual links.

13 Elastic thread
This type of thread comes in a variety of thicknesses and is great for creating designs that need to stretch over the head or hands. It can be knotted, so is easy for children to use as no clasps are required.

14 Blanks
These have flat plates with a shallow wall around the sides, which holds the clay secure. They come in many styles including, bangle (channel) blanks, ring blanks, and bezel pendant blanks.

15 Cabochons
Cabochons are made of acrylic or glass and are usually round domes used to embed into clay or to stick on the surface.

16 Dolls' house miniatures
These are perfect for making miniature food jewelry.

Polymer Clay Techniques

To work successfully with polymer clay, there are some basic techniques you will need to learn.

Conditioning polymer clay

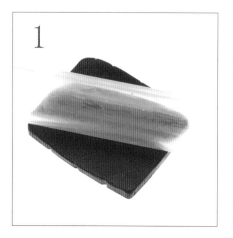

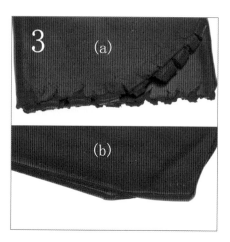

You must condition clay to make it soft and easy to use; it also makes it stronger after firing. Conditioning is often done using a pasta machine, as it saves a lot of time. If you don't have a machine then follow the steps and keep rolling out the clay with a roller on a non-stick surface.

1 Cut a piece of clay off the block using a tissue blade or craft knife that is about ¼in (6mm) thick (it is much easier to work with small pieces and combine them when they are soft). Start with a roller and roll to thin the sheet a little.

2 Place the sheet in the pasta machine on its thickest setting and roll through twice. Now fold the clay sheet in half, making sure you push the sides together starting from the fold so you don't trap air in the clay. Place the folded sheet in the pasta machine again with the fold down, so the folded edge is in line with the rollers.

3 To begin with, the edges of the clay will look broken (a), but just keep going. You will need to roll the clay at least 20 times if the clay you are using is not new. Conditioning is pretty simple, you just keep rolling and folding the clay until it's soft and the edges look smooth (b).

Mixing clay colors

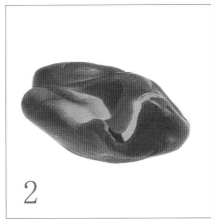

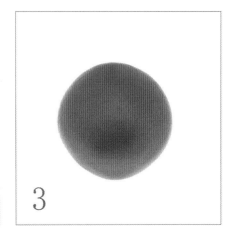

You can make polymer clay in any color that you fancy; many brands sell a wide range of colors but you can mix them and make the exact color you want. When mixing clay, only mix within the same brand of clay, as they all have different baking temperatures.

1 Measure out the clay you want to combine and roll into balls.

2 Press each color ball flat and place together, then squash them into a flat sheet. Fold the sheet in half and press together. Keep folding and pressing. Try to not add air; you may hear bubbles popping as you mix the clay.

3 Keep mixing the clay until you cannot see any marbling and the piece is one solid color.

Reducing a cane

It is impossible to make tiny canes. Instead, make them around 1in (25mm) in size and reduce to the size you want, without distoring the pattern running through the cane.

1 Take the section of cane you want to reduce. When learning to reduce canes, start with a fairly small section of cane in case it goes wrong.

2 Squeeze the clay in the middle of the cane, turn a little and squeeze again so the middle starts to reduce in size evenly. Keep squeezing until the middle is about the size you want the whole piece to be. Make sure it is even so it looks like a dumbbell. Continue to squeeze and turn the cane between your fingers, pushing out toward the end, so it starts to elongate. Don't try to stretch the cane, as that will ruin the inside pattern.

3 Chop off the ends, because they will have distorted a bit. Then, pop the cane in the fridge to harden a little; this will help prevent the cane distorting further when you slice it with a tissue blade.

Overlay blend

The overlay blend is the first of two ways we shall show you so that you can create colorful blended sheets of polymer clay. These blends are most easily made using a pasta machine, since you will be rolling out the clay multiple times. The overlay blend delivers narrow bands of color, which haze together almost electrically.

1   Condition the clay first then form several clay colors into logs and flatten them slightly with your fingertips. Lay the logs side by side, overlapping each slightly with its neighbor. Each log will become a band of color in the finished blend—so the thicker the log, the wider the band it will make. Try to use colors that contrast well with each other but still form an attractive shade when mixed.

2   Set the pasta machine to setting No.1. With the logs running vertically, feed in the clay and roll it out. Fold the resulting sheet in half, top to bottom (matching the colors). You can misalign the colors slightly for a softer finished blend or match them more closely if you prefer the blending a little crisper. Run the folded clay through the pasta machine, starting from the fold.

3   Keep folding and rolling the clay in the same way, always rolling from the fold with the lines running vertically. After several repetitions the colors will start to blend together. Stop when you are happy with the effect.

To hand roll, use an acrylic hand roller and rolling guides, taping the guides to the work surface to prevent the blend widening as you roll.

Skinner blend

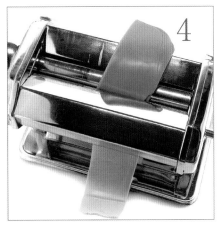

More subtle, sunset-like graduated sheets of clay can be made using the Skinner blend method, which takes its name from polymer clay artist Judith Skinner, who adapted the technique from screen printing. Skinner blends are easiest to make if using at least 1oz (25g) of each color of clay so that you have enough clay to use the whole width of the pasta machine.

1 Choose two colors of clay and condition first. You need to form right-angle triangles from two different colors of clay. Take each color in turn and roll it into a rectangular sheet (the width of the pasta machine). Cut the sheet in half diagonally, stack the two halves together and then trim into a neat triangle. When both triangles are made, align their edges to form a two-tone rectangle. Push the edges together so the two colors stick together along the diagonal line.

2 Carefully fold the rectangle in half from top to bottom, so the fold runs horizontally. Set the pasta machine to the No.1 setting and roll the clay, always placing the folded edge into the rollers first. Fold the clay in half again, folding top to bottom as before. Starting from the fold again, roll the clay through the pasta machine. Continue folding and rolling, always folding the sheet top to bottom and rolling it from the fold.

3 After several repetitions, the sheet will take on a banded appearance. Continue rolling and folding until the bands of color start to blend together. When the sheet appears seamlessly blended, give it a few more passes through the pasta machine just for luck! Expect to do about 20 passes through the pasta machine.

4 If making canes, try lengthening the blend first. Select a thinner setting on the pasta machine. Fold the Skinner blend in half top to bottom as before, but this time feed it through the machine narrow end first. The resulting clay ribbon can be spiraled up for making bullseye and leaf canes. Alternatively, fold it up accordion-style and compress into a block for use in geometric or striped canes.

Based on information from Emma Ralph, UK beadmaker

Jewelry Techniques

Two basic jewelry techniques will enable
you to turn your polymer clay into jewelry.

Opening and closing a jumpring

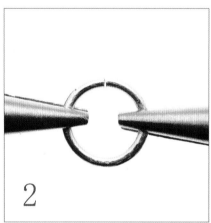

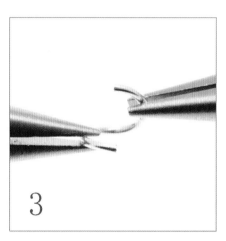

To make sure that jumprings shut securely, it is important to know how to open and close them correctly. You will need two pairs of pliers with flat jaws—chain-nose, flat-nose or nylon-nose will work.

1   Take a jumpring in two pairs of pliers with the opening centered at the top. Holding the jumpring this way—with one pair of pliers across one side of the ring—helps to stabilize large rings.

2   You can also hold the pliers this way with both pairs facing inward. Both ways are fine and the way you need to attach the jumpring often dictates which way you hold it.

3   Hold the jumping on both sides and twist one hand toward you and the other hand away. This will keep the ring round in shape. Reverse the action to close the ring. Don't ever pull the ring apart as that will warp the shape. Use this technique to open loops on eyepins too.

Making a simple loop

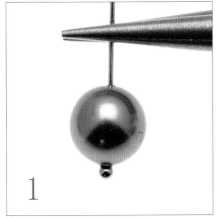

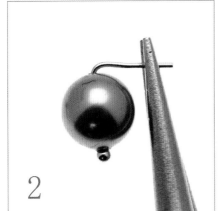

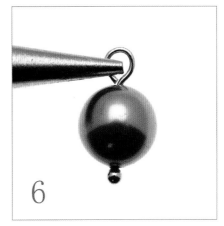

Loops have a multitude of functions in making jewelry so forming them properly is a skill worth mastering. A simple (sometimes called open) loop can be opened and closed to allow them to be attached and detached as desired.

1 Thread the bead onto a head- or eyepin and cut the pin about ⅜in (10mm) above the bead.

2 Bend the wire to a right angle above the bead.

3 Using round-nose pliers, grasp the wire at the very end and curl it around the plier jaws.

4 Roll the wire around to meet the bead.

5 Move the plier jaws around the loop to sit by the bead, away from the open end. Bend the loop back to sit directly above the bead.

6 Use chain-nose pliers to tighten the loop by wiggling it until the gap is closed.

If you find that pliers mark the jumprings, wrap a bit of masking tape around the ends.

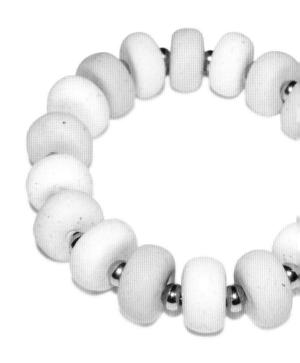

Summer
Sweets

These beautiful pieces of jewelry capture the essence of the summer months and will sparkle in the light. Alison Gallant has used a simple color combination to give this easy-to-make set a classic look.

FOR THE NECKLACE YOU WILL NEED

1 block Premo! Sculpey Accents White Granite (5061)

1 block Premo! Sculpey Accents Translucent (5310)

Tiny pieces of Premo! Sculpey Accents Peacock Pearl (5038), Wasabi (5022), Orange (5033), Fuchsia (5504), Purple (5513)

Tissue blade or craft knife

Alcohol inks (optional)

Pasta machine

⅝in (16mm) round cutter

Needle tool

Superfine wet/dry sandpaper

Coarse cloth such as denim

Nylon-coated beading wire

30 x 4mm silver-colored spacer beads

Side cutters

2 x silver-colored crimps

1 x trigger clasp

Chain-nose pliers

1 x 5mm jumpring

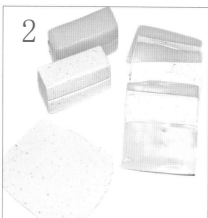

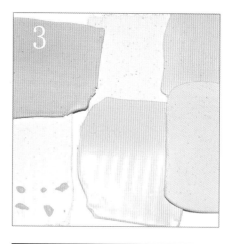

Necklace

1 To make the beads for the necklace the White Granite and Translucent clays are combined with a little color added. The clays have very different textures. White Granite contains "gold" flecks that mimic the look of pebbles or just add a beautiful sparkle to the finish. The Translucent clay adds depth and a sheen.

2 Condition the clays. This can be done by hand, but you can use the pasta machine for speed. Take each block of the White Granite and Translucent clays, slice and roll the sheets through the pasta machine at setting No.1 (see page 16).

3 Divide into six roughly equal-sized pieces. Decide on the colors of your beads and add tiny amounts of color to five of the White Granite and Translucent mixes, leaving one white. Mix thoroughly and adjust amount of color to suit your preference.

4 You can create a similar finish to the clay by using alcohol inks, but they can be messy, especially when using several colors. An alternative effect is to finely chop or grate the color and roughly mix to create a marbled look.

5 The tiny pieces of color, White Granite and Translucent mix need to be thoroughly blended before using the pasta machine. Then roll the sheets through the pasta machine at setting No.1. Stamp out 15 x ⅝in (16mm) circles from each sheet.

6 Working with three circles at a time, roll 30 balls of clay. These can be as near to perfect as you can make them or flattened slightly to make a more interesting shape. Pierce each one through the center or the longer side with a needle tool. Bake according to the clay manufacturer's instructions.

7 Sand the beads with superfine sandpaper. Buff to a shine using coarse cloth or denim.

8 Decide on the order of your beads, either in a sequence, or randomly as you pick them up. A true random pattern usually looks best in this sort of necklace as long as you do not have two of the same colors together.

9 Cut a length of beading wire with the side cutters and thread on the polymer beads with a silver-colored spacer in between each one. To finish the necklace, thread on a crimp bead and the clasp, and loop the beading wire back through the crimp. Pull until you have a small loop with the clasp on it. Squash the crimp flat with chain-nose pliers. Repeat for the other end adding the jumpring instead of the clasp.

Earrings

YOU WILL NEED

Polymer clay in two colors of your choice

2 x silver-colored washers

2 x 2in (50mm) headpins

2 x silver-colored earwires

Make two round beads about ⅝in (15mm) across and two smaller beads about ⅜in (10mm), thread onto headpins, with a silver-colored washer in between. Turn simple loops (see page 21) in the headpins and attach to earwires using chain- or flat-nose pliers. Open the loop on the earwire by twisting the loop to one side (do not pull it outward) and thread on the headpin. Close the loop by twisting it back in line with the earwire.

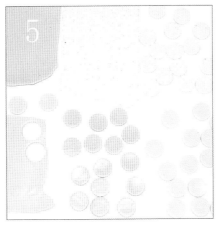

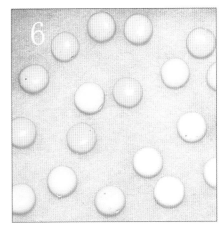

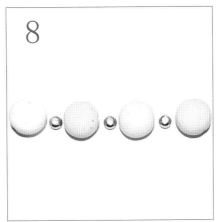

Bracelet

YOU WILL NEED

Premo! Sculpey Accents
White Granite (5061)

Premo! Sculpey Accents
Translucent (5310)

Tiny pieces of Premo! Sculpey
Peacock Pearl (5038), Wasabi
(5022), Orange (5033), Fuchsia
(5504), Purple (5513)

15 x 4mm silver-colored spacer beads

20 x ½in (500 x 1mm) elastic thread

Use the same techniques as you used for the necklace to make 15
small beads. Stamp out 15 x ⅜in (10mm) circles from each sheet
to make the beads. This time flatten the beads so they are more like
flat discs. Thread them onto elastic with contrasting spacer beads in
between. Tie the ends and hide the knot inside a spacer bead.

For a simpler finish,
make the holes in
the beads bigger
and thread on your
choice of ribbon
or silk.

Garland Petals

These pretty, petal-like elasticated pieces by Alison Gallant have a strong resemblance to a beautiful Hawaiian garland. This easy-to-wear set utilizes a striking blend of pearly colors.

FOR THE BRACELET
YOU WILL NEED

½ block Premo! Sculpey Accents Blue Pearl (5289)

½ block Premo! Sculpey Accents Bright Green Pearl (5035)

½ block Premo! Sculpey Accents Peacock Pearl (5038)

Tissue blade or craft knife

Pasta machine

Sheet of blank copy paper

¹³⁄₁₆in (20mm) round cutter

Needle tool

Wet/dry sandpaper (optional)

Coarse cloth such as denim (optional)

¹⁄₃₂in (1mm) clear elastic cord

Size 6 (4mm) seed beads

Earrings

YOU WILL NEED

Leftover blend from main project

⅜in (10mm) round cutter

2 x 2in (50mm) silver-colored headpins

2 x silver-colored earwires

10 x size 6 (4mm) silver seed beads

Reduce the blend, setting to No.4 or No.5 on the pasta machine. Stamp out 12 circles using the cutter, pinch to make petals as before, and bake. Place on two headpins with a tiny silver bead between each petal. Turn loops (see page 21) and add earwires.

Bracelet

1 Condition the clay. Roll half a block of Blue Pearl, Bright Green Pearl, and Peacock Pearl through the pasta machine at setting No.1 (see page 16). Form into double thickness rectangles about 2½in x 4¾in (60 x 120mm). Cut the Blue Pearl in half lengthwise. Fold a piece of blank copy paper into a concertina with at least four channels to hold the beads in place for baking.

2 Lay the clay sheets on your tile in the following order: Blue Pearl, Peacock Pearl, Bright Green Pearl, and Blue Pearl. Overlap them by ⅜in (10mm) and roll over lightly to join together. Roll through the pasta machine at setting No.1. Fold from bottom to the top and repeat about 20 times until you have a well-blended sheet. This is called an overlay blend (see page 18).

3 Cut the sheet in half across the width. Turn one piece 90 degrees, reduce pasta machine thickness by one setting and roll through again. Lay the clay on the board and stamp out 32 x ¹³⁄₁₆in (20mm) diameter circles. Leave them exactly where they are.

4 Take each circle in turn and carefully fold the edges of one side together and pinch to make a petal shape. Use the needle tool to make a hole through the pinched part, large enough for the elastic to go through. Gently curl over (back a little) the front edge of the petal.

5 Fold, pinch, and curl each petal in turn across the color blend and place the wide part down in paper channels, keeping them in order. Bake the clay according to the manufacturer's instructions.

6 The beads will naturally have a pearly, satin finish. They can be sanded and buffed but it is a lot of extra work! Keeping them in order, string 32 onto the clear elastic with a seed bead between each one for extra sparkle. This fits around a 7½in (190mm) wrist snugly. Finish the elastic with a double knot.

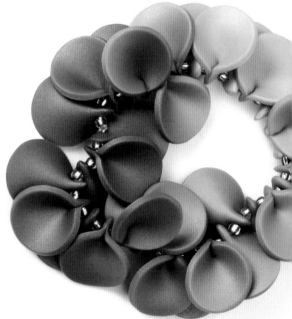

This method of creating petals is an easy way to make shapes from clay. Form and perfect them before you bake so that there is no difficult carving or drilling involved.

1

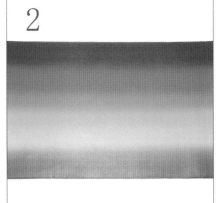

2

3

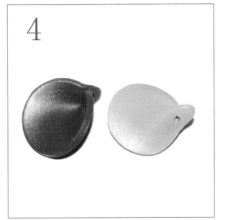

4

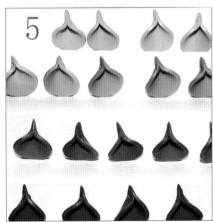

5

6

Necklace

YOU WILL NEED

Leftover blend from
main project

Ready-made silver-colored
fine-chain necklace

5 x 6mm jumprings

5 x 5mm jumprings

Stamp out 5 x $^{13}/_{16}$in (20mm)
circles across the remaining
blend. Pinch one side to make
the petals, drill through the
pinch, and bake. Measure
along the chain and add 5mm
jumprings at suitable intervals
(see page 20). Attach 6mm
jumprings to the petals and join
onto the 5mm rings.

Try not to get fingerprints on the clay.
Remove them carefully with the side
of your finger if you do. You can wear
gloves if necessary.

Pretty Poppies

Nina Fletcher's striking collection is inspired by delicate poppies. They are simple to make, and are the perfect way to give your outfits a fresh new look.

FOR THE PENDANT YOU WILL NEED

½ block Premo! Sculpey in three base colors

½ block Premo! Sculpey White (5001) or Accents Pearl (5101)

⅛ block Premo! Sculpey Black (5042)

Pasta machine

3 x round cutters, about ¹³⁄₁₆in (20mm), 1³⁄₁₆in (30mm), 2in (50mm)

5 x metal/glass beads

10 x small beads

Metallic pen

Liquid polymer clay

US 18 gauge (SWG 19, 1mm) beading wire

Side cutters

10 x crimps

Chain-nose pliers

2 x cord ends

1 x clasp

2 x 6mm jumprings

These flowers can also look great as cufflinks. Just make the flowers smaller and attach to cufflink blanks.

Necklace

1 Using your base colors blend one-third of each color with White or Pearl clay and one-third with a tiny bit of Black clay. Mix some of the base colors together to make more variations, until you have a palette. Condition the clay. Roll through each layer on the pasta machine between setting No.3 and No.4 (see page 16). If you would like contrasting color layers, roll out multiple thickness sheets in each color and make the top layer thicker to take the center bead.

2 Cut out five circles from the thicker sheets with the smallest cutter and form these around your chosen center beads. Stretch and shape the clay gently using your fingers to form the flower's wavy edges. You can bake the flowers resting on top of the cutters (the center of the flower will rest inside the cutter and the edge of the flower will be on the cutter) to help them keep a three-dimensional shape. Bake according to the clay manufacturer's instructions.

3 Paint the edges of the flowers with the metallic pen and then leave to dry. Cut out the next size circles. Dab liquid polymer clay on the baked pieces and place them onto the newly cut circles. Stretch and shape the new layer, then bake.

4 Paint the edges with metallic pen and leave to dry. Choose your color combination for the three large flowers. Coat the underneath of the baked pieces with liquid polymer clay. Using the largest cutter, cut out the three circles. Stretch and shape as in previous steps. Attach them to their corresponding pieces, then reshape if necessary. Bake as before. When cool, paint the final layers with a metallic pen and leave to dry.

5 Condition the clay to make the bails. Roll a sheet out on a pasta machine on setting No.2 or No.3. Cut ¼ x 1⅛in (6 x 30mm) strips for each bail. Cut off sections of beading wire to form the channels in the bails. Place the sections on the strip, fold the strip over, and cut the edge at a 45-degree angle. Use liquid polymer clay to "glue" the bails to the backs of the flowers so that the wire sits about ⅜in (10mm) from the top. Bake again.

6 Cut the beading wire to your desired length. Thread small beads on either side of the flower pieces; this protects the clay from the sharpness of the crimps. Then thread the crimps on either side of the small beads. Arrange the five flowers as desired on the wire then carefully squash the crimps closed with the chain-nose pliers. Finish each end with cord ends and add a clasp to one cord end with a jumpring (see page 20). Add a final jumpring to the other cord end.

Brooch

YOU WILL NEED

Small amount of polymer clay in two or three colors

Liquid polymer clay

1 x metal/glass bead or beadcap

Metallic pen

1 x brooch bar

Two-part epoxy resin

The brooch is made in the same way as the main project following steps 1–4. Make your brooch with either two or three layers as desired and color the edges with a metallic pen. Take the brooch bar and glue to the back of the flower with two-part epoxy resin.

Use a cloth such as linen to make a texture on the surface of the sheets before cutting the circles. This will give a different finish to the flowers.

Ring

YOU WILL NEED

Small amount of polymer clay in two or three colors

Liquid polymer clay

1 x metal/glass bead or beadcap

Metallic pen

1 x ring blank and flat pad

Two-part epoxy resin

Follow the steps of the main project to make a flower for a ring. The necklace-sized flowers will make a large feature ring (or you can use smaller diameter cutters to make a smaller ring). You can also try using a smaller bead or beadcap for the center. Make your ring with either two or three layers as desired and color the edges with a metallic pen. Take the ring blank and glue to the back of the flower with two-part epoxy resin.

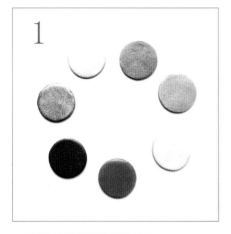

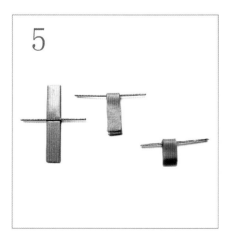

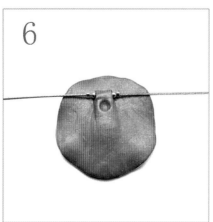

Floral Art

Create your own secret garden with this stunning floral art collection of jewelry by Alison Gallant. You can have fun combining the colors to make a themed set.

FOR THE PENDANT YOU WILL NEED

½ block Premo! Sculpey Purple (5513)

½ block Premo! Sculpey Turquoise (5505)

½ block Premo! Sculpey Blush (5020)

2 x blocks Premo! Sculpey White (5001)

Small piece Premo! Sculpey Accents Translucent (5310)

2 x blocks Premo! Sculpey Black (5042)

Pasta machine

Tissue blade or craft knife

Needle tool

Wet/dry sandpaper

Sheet of blank copy paper

2¼in (55mm) flower cutter

Straw

Coarse cloth such as denim

Ready-made silver-colored chain necklace

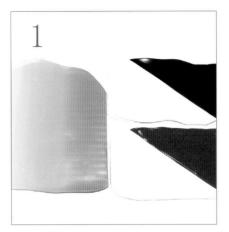

1

2

3

4

5

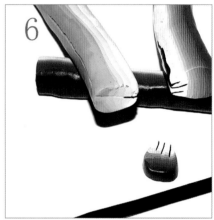

6

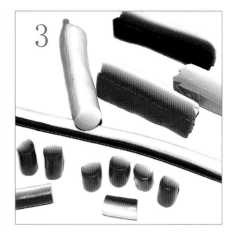

7

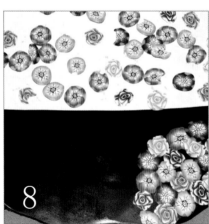

8

9

Pendant

1　Use half a block of Purple, Turquoise, and Blush clays to create three offset Skinner blends (see page 19). White clay is used with each color. Roll the clays through the pasta machine at setting No.1 (see page 16). They should be blended across the sheets, with a band of solid color on one side and white on the other.

2　Turn each blend 90 degrees, then fold in half lengthwise. With the white edge first, pass through the pasta machine three times, reducing the thickness by one setting each time. Starting with the colored end, press ¾in (18mm) onto your work surface, then fold the clay back over and pleat back and forth. Gently press the layers together.

3　Cut each stack in half lengthways. Using one piece of each color blend, round the long edges, then roll each stack to 8in (200mm). Cut in half. Slice one section into four equal pieces and the other into five. Reduce the five to 1in (25mm) in diameter (see page 17).

4　Take one of each of the four thicker pieces, flatten it with your fingers and form into a jellyroll with white on the outside. This is the center of the rose. Flatten the colored side of the remaining three pieces and pinch the top edges, leaving the white domed. Place the three petals around the center, with white sides out and overlapping each other.

5　Form the remaining five pieces into teardrop shapes and place around the rose, again overlapping them with white sides out. With a needle tool, make an indent along each petal to give a natural look. Roll a thin snake of Translucent clay and press into the gaps between and along the petals to help retain the shape when the canes are reduced.

6　Round the long edges of the second stacks and form into a petal shape. Make three cuts along the length, through the White and just into the color. Roll a quarter block of Black through the pasta machine at setting No.4 or 5 and make slices to fit into the cuts. Press back together. Place a strip of Black on one side of each petal shape from the base to where the White meets the color.

7　Reduce the canes made in Step 6 to 9½in (240mm) and cut in to six. Roll a one-eighth block of White into a log 1¼in (28mm) high. Roll a sheet of Black through setting No.1 on the pasta machine and wrap around the White. Reduce to 8¼in (210mm), cut into seven and press together. Position the petals around the Black and White center. Form a one-eighth block of Translucent into a ⅜in (10mm) round log. Cut into five, then four sections lengthways. Place a piece between the petals of each blend.

Earrings

YOU WILL NEED

Selection of unbaked flower canes (as in main project)

Small piece Premo! Sculpey Black (5042)

2 x silver-colored earwires

2 x 6mm jumprings

Stamp out two ¾in (19mm) flower shapes and make a hole near to the top of one of the petals. When baked, cooled, and sanded insert jumprings (see page 20) through the holes. Add the earwires before closing the jumprings.

Bracelet

YOU WILL NEED

Selection of unbaked flower canes (as in main project)

Small piece Premo! Sculpey Black (5042)

1 x clasp

8 x 6mm jumprings

Using a 1¼in (31mm) flower cutter, stamp out seven pieces and make holes in the top and bottom petals of each flower. When baked, cooled, and sanded link together with large jumprings (see page 20). Add a clasp to the final jumpring on one end. Add a jumpring on the other end for the clasp to attach to.

8　Reduce all six canes to just over ⅜in (10mm) in diameter. Roll a block of Black through the pasta machine at setting No.1 and place on a sheet of coarse sandpaper. This will texture the back. Take wafer-thin slices from the canes and lay on the clay. After every five or six slices, lay paper over the top and smooth it in with your fingers so you can't feel any bumps.

9　Stamp out the required shapes. Use a 2¼in (55mm) flower cutter and a straw for cutting a hole for stringing. Bake on the sandpaper, according to the clay manufacturer's instructions. Sand the front and sides lightly with fine grade sandpaper. Buff to a shine using coarse cloth or denim and string on the ready-made chain necklace.

Spring Snowdrops

Lynn Allingham celebrates the arrival of spring by capturing a delicate snowdrop of polymer clay in a bottle. Teamed with pretty matching jewelry pieces, this set is a unique way to welcome the warmer days.

FOR THE PENDANT YOU WILL NEED

Fimo Classic in White

Fimo Classic in Leaf Green

Fimo Classic in Green

Fimo Classic in Chocolate

3 x 4–5mm uncoated beads

Tissue blade or craft knife

4 x gunmetal-colored headpins

Needle tool

Liquid polymer clay

Two-part epoxy resin

1½in x ⅞in (38 x 22mm) miniature glass bottle

1 x gunmetal-colored puffy heart charm

18in (460mm) length of gunmetal-colored 2mm trace chain

1 x gunmetal-colored trigger clasp

1 x 6mm jumpring

2 x 7mm gunmetal-colored jumprings

Wire cutter

Round-nose pliers

Flat-nose or chain-nose pliers

Earrings

YOU WILL NEED

Leftover pieces of Fimo Classic in White and Leaf Green

2 x green size 2 (4mm) bugle beads

2 x green size 6 (4mm) seed beads

2⅜in (60mm) x 2mm gunmetal-colored trace chain

2 x 2in (50mm) gunmetal-colored ball-ended headpins

2 x gunmetal-colored ear posts with loop

Follow Steps 1–2 in the main project to make four snowdrop flowers. Bake and when cool thread each flower onto a ball-ended headpin. Add a seed bead and bugle bead then make a simple loop (see page 21) above and attach one to either end of the trace chain. Open the loop on the ear posts (twist gently to one side with chain-nose pliers) and attach the chain about one-third of the way along. When the earrings hang the flowers are at a different length. Close the loop on the post when you are happy with how the earrings look.

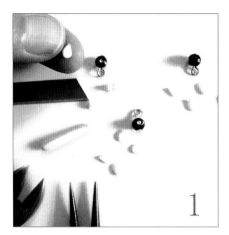

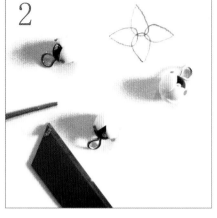

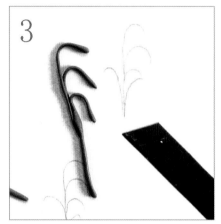

Handle the clay as little as possible. Use tiny paper wedges to hold the delicate pieces in position when baking.

Pendant

1 Take the White clay and roll into a cylinder and cut into small discs. Take each disc and soften and shape between your finger and thumb to create petal shapes. You will need four petals per flower. Now thread three small, uncoated beads onto a headpin. Cut and create a simple loop (see page 21). These beads will provide a base shape for your snowdrops.

2 Assemble the petals onto the beads. Lay out the petals, overlapping each other. Lay the petals on top of the beads and gently pat into place with the tips of the petals pointing downward. Take a small amount of Leaf Green clay and roll into a cylinder about ⅟₃₂in (1mm) thick. Cut tiny discs with a tissue blade or craft knife and gently add to the tip of each petal.

3 Take three pieces of Leaf Green clay and roll out into long thin stems about ⅟₃₂in (1mm) thick. Leave the tips slightly wider as this is where they will connect to the flowers. Arrange the three thin stems into a curved ascending order. Gently smooth together the base of the stems to create a thicker end. The total length of stem should be up to 1in (25mm).

4 Take the Leaf Green and the Green clay and fashion into three long leaf shapes between your fingers and thumb and attach these as desired to the base of the stem. Gently remove the flowers from the beads and attach to each of the three stems by gently pushing to connect them. Very carefully arrange the flowers as desired, taking care not to distort them. Bake according to the clay manufacturer's instructions.

5 To make the base, take a small ball of Chocolate clay and flatten slightly. Distress the top of the base with a pin and make a hole in the center thick enough for the stem to slot into using a needle tool. At this point check that the base will fit easily into the top of the glass bottle. Varnish the baked flowers lightly with liquid polymer clay. Bake both items together.

6 Glue the flower stem into the base with two-part epoxy resin and let dry. Add glue to the bottom of the glass bottle and gently put your plant into position. Push a headpin through the cork, thread the puffy heart charm on, and cut and loop the pin. Glue the cork all the way round, push into place, and leave to dry. Attach the trigger clasp to one end of the chain using the 6mm jumpring and add a 7mm jumpring to the other end of the chain. Finally add the bottle top to the chain with a 7mm jumpring (see page 20).

Polymer clay is quite flexible after baking and the flower stems will withstand a small amount of movement when being put into the miniature bottle.

Ring

YOU WILL NEED

Leftover pieces of Fimo Classic in White and Leaf Green

30 x white size 8 (3mm) seed beads

30 x green size 6 (4mm) seed beads

2⅜in (6cm) x 2mm gunmetal-colored trace chain

34 x 1in (25mm) gunmetal-colored ball-ended headpins

1 x 10 loop gunmetal-colored ring blank

Follow Steps 1–2 in the main project to make four snowdrop flowers. Bake and when cool, thread each one onto a ball-ended headpin and make a simple loop at the end (see page 21). Take the green and white seed beads and thread two onto a ball-headed pin, cut and loop. Make 30 of these. Take one beaded headpin at a time and open the loop by twisting the loop gently sideways, link it onto a loop on the ring and close. Repeat with all the other headpins, attaching three to each loop. Randomly add in the snowdrop flowers.

Beautiful Blooms

These stunning roses were designed by Alison Gallant. Following her inspiration you can create delicate, feminine jewelry centered around these gorgeous summer flowers.

FOR THE NECKLACE YOU WILL NEED

½ block Premo! Sculpey Fuchsia (5504)

⅟₁₆ block Premo! Sculpey Cadmium Red Hue (5382)

½ block Premo! Sculpey Accents Pearl (5101)

¾ block Premo! Sculpey White (5001)

¼ block Premo! Sculpey Accents Peacock Pearl (5038)

Pasta machine

Round cutters in ¾₁₆in (20mm), ¾in (18mm), ⅝in (16mm), ⁹⁄₁₆in (14mm), and ½in (12mm)

Clay shaper

Needle tool

Texture sponge

Wet/dry sandpaper

Two-part epoxy resin

2 x 7mm jumprings

Chain-nose pliers

3ft (1m) faux suede cord

2 x ribbon crimps

1 x clasp

Necklace

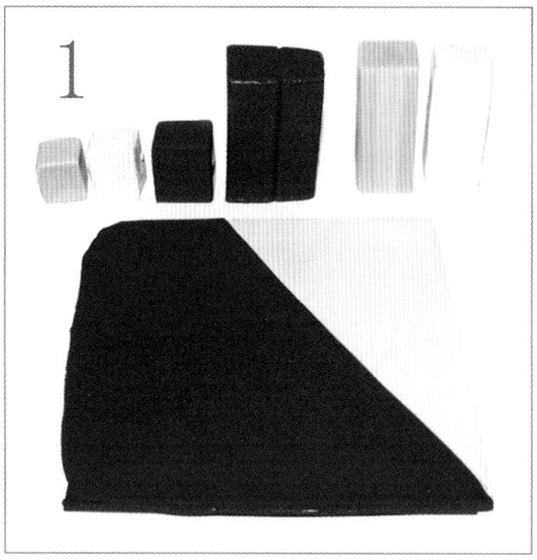

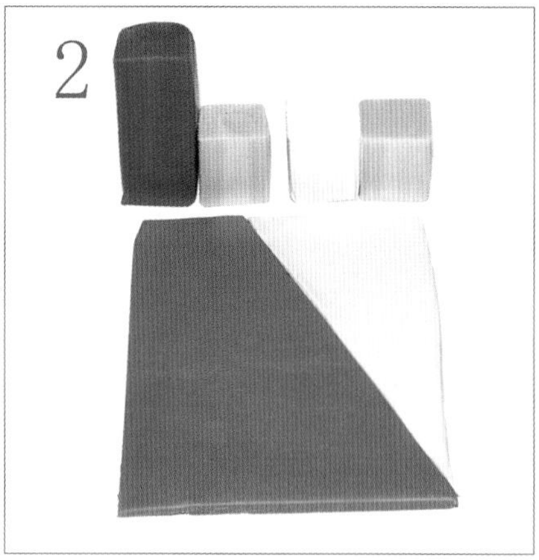

1 Mix 1/2 block of Fuchsia, 1/16 block of Cadmium Red Hue, 1/16 block of White and 1/32 block of Pearl, and for the white side, 1/4 block of White and 1/4 block of Pearl. Roll both out on the pasta machine at setting No.1 (see page 16), to form into a Skinner blend (see page 19).

2 Next, mix 1/4 block of Peacock Pearl and 1/8 block of Pearl to lighten the color. Then mix together 1/8 block of White and 1/8 block of Pearl. Roll out on a pasta machine at setting No.2 or No.3 to form into a Skinner blend as in Step 1.

3 Roll each Skinner blend through a pasta machine about 20 times, folding from the bottom to the top after each pass. Place both blended sheets on your work tile. You should see dark, medium, and light shades across the blends.

4 Begin with the pink blend, stamp out four 3/4in (18mm) circles from the darkest part of the sheet, leaving the clay on the tile. Then, with a 13/16in (20mm) cutter, stamp out three circles from the middle of the blend and finally five 13/16in (20mm) circles from the lightest part.

5 Carefully lift the rest of the blended sheet. Fold and roll it into another sheet on setting No.3. or No.4 on the pasta machine, keeping the original blend, and place on a tile. From the turquoise sheet, cut out eight 5/8in (16mm) circles from the dark area, six 3/4in (18mm) from the medium area, and ten 3/4in (18mm) circles from the lightest part of the blend.

6 Using the pieces from Step 4, take one of the dark pink 3/4in (18mm) circles, flatten and thin one edge with your finger or a clay shaper. Curve the center round on itself, keeping the thin edge at the top. This is the center of the rose.

7 Flatten one edge of the three dark circles and attach to the center, thin edge up. Use a finger, clay shaper or a needle tool to flare the edges and indent to give a natural look. Repeat with the next set of three and finally the five lighter petals.

8 Repeat with the turquoise blend to form two roses. Then stamp out eight 1/2in (12mm) dark, six 9/16in (14mm) medium, and ten 9/16in (14mm) light circles from the remaining pink sheet. Form two roses. Trim the bases flat. Bake according to the clay manufacturer's instructions.

9 Mix the remainder of the pink sheet and roll through the pasta machine at setting No.1. Create texture with a sponge. Cut out a base in a "U" or "V" shape to act as a base for the roses. Pierce each end as shown in the main image on page 42. Bake and cool. Sand the untextured side with fine sandpaper. Position the roses and stick with two-part epoxy resin. Add a jumpring (see page 20) to each end of the base and thread through the suede cord. Cut to your desired length then place both cord ends into a ribbon crimp and squeeze the crimp closed with chain-nose pliers. Add a clasp to the ribbon crimp on one end with a jumpring and a single jumpring to the other ribbon crimp.

Bracelet

YOU WILL NEED

Leftover pieces of Premo! Sculpey colors from the main project

6 x 8mm jumprings

1 x large link chain bracelet with clasp

Follow Steps 1–3 of the main project to make a pink Skinner blend. Form six rosebuds, following Step 6. Pierce the bases with a needle tool and make sure the hole can take an 8mm jumpring. Bake the roses and attach to a silver chain bracelet with the jumprings (see page 20).

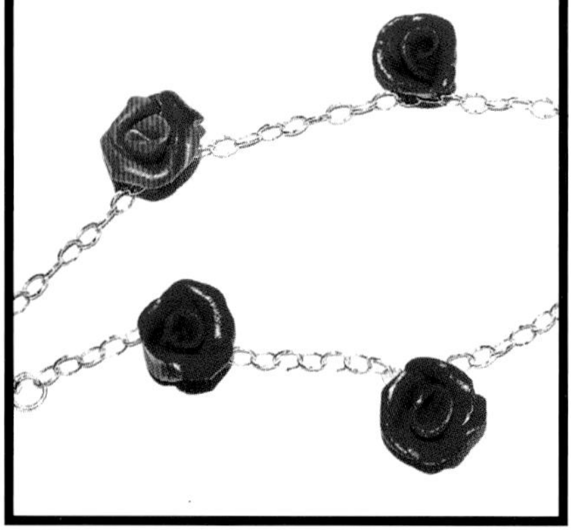

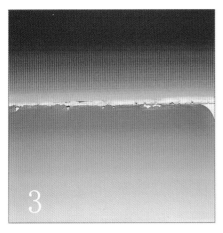

3

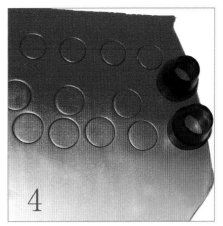

4

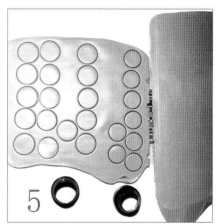

5

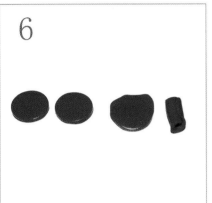

6

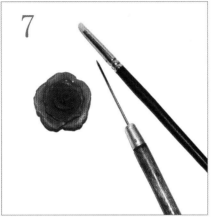

7

8

9

Adding one layer of petals at a time, tweaking and pinching them to give a natural look, results in a unique rose that can grace a neck, top a cake, or dress a table.

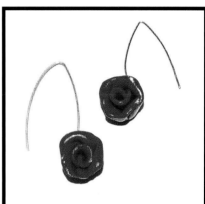

Earrings

YOU WILL NEED

1in (25mm) block of Premo! Sculpey colors from the main project

2 x 3in (76mm) lengths of US 20-gauge (SWG 21, 0.8mm) wire

Follow Steps 1–3 of the main project. Form two tiny rosebuds by cutting four ½in (12mm) circles, curling the first one to make the center, and slightly flattening the others to make petals. Take the pieces of wire and push into the roses. Bake these in position and cool. Remove the wire and stick back in place with two-part epoxy resin. With a small piece of sandpaper, round off the ends of the wire, then bend into a curve with round-nose pliers.

Golden Deco

Lynn Allingham combines 1930s Art Deco floral art with fashionable geometric shapes and bold, sophisticated colors. These feminine designs create a stylish set of modern jewelry.

FOR THE PENDANT YOU WILL NEED

Fimo Soft in White

Fimo Soft in Black

Craft rolling pin

Tissue blade or craft knife

Fine brush

Fimo Accessories gold powder

Needle tool

Liquid polymer clay

Pin vise and drill bits

1m (3ft) gold-colored 2mm trace chain

1 x gold-colored trigger clasp

6 x gold-colored ball-headed pins

1 x gold-colored fancy headpin

1 x decorative gold-colored bead

6 x 4mm black crystal bicone beads

7 x 3mm gold-colored beads

7 x 3mm silver crystal bicone beads

1 x gray large glass crystal

18in (460mm) gold-colored curb chain

9 x 4mm gold-colored jumprings

2 x 3mm gold-colored jumprings

Round-nose pliers

Flat-nose pliers

Side cutters

Pendant

1. Roll a piece of White clay between your hands until it is soft. Using a small craft rolling pin, roll out the clay until it is about ⅛in (3mm) thick. Neatly cut a triangular shape, roughly 1¼in (28mm) in length using a tissue blade or craft knife. Press downward into the clay rather than drag the blade across.

2. Create calla lilies by rolling a small ball of White clay. Flatten it out into a thin circle, then neatly roll it from one edge to the other. To create the peak of the lily, gently pinch the clay. To create the inside stem, make thin cylinders and cut to size. To make the calla leaves, roll cylinders, then cut and flatten them between your fingers.

3. Once the flowers and leaves are made, carefully arrange them on the triangle in a formation you are happy with. Be careful not to handle the clay too much, so that the clay doesn't become distorted. Take a soft fine brush and liberally apply the gold powder. Leave the underside of the triangle white.

4. Take a large piece of Black clay, condition it and roll it out until it is about ⅛in (3mm) thick. Very carefully place the gold triangle on top of the black clay and cut the top line flush to the edge of the triangle. Cut the other two sides leaving a ³⁄₁₆in (4mm) border. Create seven evenly spaced holes in the black border and two in the top corners using a needle tool.

5. Bake according to the manufacturer's instructions. Once cool, varnish gently with liquid polymer clay, bake again and cool. Gently drill the holes back in using a ¹⁄₃₂in (1mm) drill piece. Cut seven pieces of trace chain 1⅛in (29mm) in length. Assemble six ball-headed pins with color coordinating beads. The middle pin can be more elaborate to create a feature, such as a large crystal on a fancy headpin.

6. Cut and loop (see page 21) all the beaded pins using round-nose pliers. Attach the pins to the chains and attach the chains to the pendant using 4mm jumprings (see page 20). Add three links of chunky curb chain to the two top holes using jumprings. Use an 18in (460mm) chain for the pendant to hang from and attach to the curb chain using 3mm jumprings.

Earrings

YOU WILL NEED

Leftover pieces of Fimo Soft from main project

Fimo Accessories gold powder

2 x 2½in (60mm) 2mm gold-colored trace chains

6 x 4mm gold-colored jumprings

2 x gold-colored earwires

2 x 1in (25mm) gold-colored ball-headed pins

2 x 4mm black crystal bicone beads

2 x 3mm gold-colored beads

2 x 3mm silver crystal bicone beads

Create matching Art Deco earrings following the steps in the main project. Just make the triangle piece smaller and with one flower per earring. Place the flowers in the opposite direction on the two pieces. Make a hole in each corner of the black triangle borders. Bake and cool. Take a 2½in (60mm) piece of trace chain and attach to the triangle with jumprings. Find the middle of the chain and attach an earwire. Make a single dangle of beads using Step 5 of the main project to hang in the center at the bottom of the earrings.

When rolling out polymer clay, use a craft rolling pin to get a smooth, even surface.

Adapt to current fashion trends by using bold colors and try different geometric shapes.

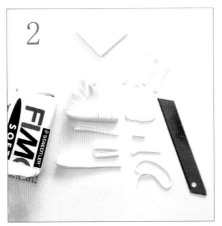

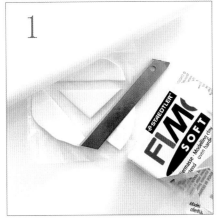

Ring

YOU WILL NEED

Leftover pieces of Fimo Soft from main project

Fimo Accessories gold powder

1 x gold-colored ring blank with flat pad

1 x 4mm gold-colored jumprings

1 x 1in (25mm) gold-colored ball-headed pins

1 x 3mm silver crystal bicone beads

Two-part epoxy resin

Create a matching Art Deco ring using the steps in the main project. This ring consists of a small square clay design mounted on a gold-colored adjustable ring blank. Make the gold flower top piece on a square of Black clay, create one hole under the flower and bake. When cool, glue the top piece to a ring blank using two-part epoxy resin. Place the crystal on the headpin and make a loop (see page 21) at the top, open the jumpring (see page 20) and place the headpin on the ring. Then thread the jumpring through the hole on the polymer square and close the ring.

Flower Power

A simple two-layer flower design made from leather by Alison Gallant translates well into this lovely matching set of jewelry. The vibrant colors chosen for these pieces make an eye-catching statement.

FOR THE BANGLE YOU WILL NEED

½ block Premo! Sculpey Cadmium Red Hue (5382)

¾ block Premo! Sculpey Ecru (5093)

½ block Premo! Sculpey Fuchsia (5504)

¼ block Premo! Sculpey Cobalt Blue (5063)

1 block Premo! Sculpey White (5001)

¹⁄₁₆ block Premo! Sculpey Cadmium Yellow Hue (5572)

¼ block Premo! Sculpey Peacock Pearl (5038)

¼ block Premo! Sculpey Jungle (5535)

Pasta machine

Tissue blade or craft knife

1 x silver-colored channel bangle

Texture sponge

Flower-shaped cutters

8 x small spacer beads

Polyester batting

Two-part epoxy resin

Necklace

YOU WILL NEED

Leftover clay from main project

Needle tool

3in (75mm) length of silver-colored chain

3 x 6mm jumprings

2 x small spacer beads

1 x ready-made silver-colored chain necklace

Pliers

Make two larger flowers following the steps for the main project, but make a small hole in each flower with a needle tool, then bake. When cool, attach a 6mm jumpring (see page 20) to a flower and add on the end link of the 3in (75mm) chain. Attach the other end of the chain to the other flower with another 6mm jumpring. With the final jumpring, attach the short chain to the chain necklace in the center opposite the clasp.

1

2

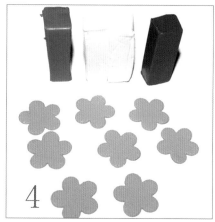

3

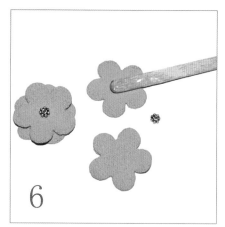

4

5

6

When baking a delicate curved polymer piece in the oven, support it with plenty of polyester batting.

Bangle

1 Different colors of clay can be mixed easily to replicate more unusual colors. Here are three blends for some of the best color mixes. The first is Cayenne, a hot, spicy red. Use ½ block of Cadmium Red and ¾ block of Ecru. Mix until fully blended on a pasta machine or by hand.

2 Roll out a sheet about 9in (240mm) by 1in (25mm) at setting No.4 or No.5 (see page 16) on the pasta machine and place in the channel of the bangle. Trim to fit and lightly texture with a sponge, especially over the join. Take eight tiny silver-colored spacers, roll a very thin snake of Cayenne, and cut pieces to fill the center holes.

3 To mix Radiant Orchid, a pink/mauve shade, use ⅝ block of Fuchsia, ¼ block of Cobalt Blue, ½ block White, and ⅟₁₆ block of Cadmium Yellow. Roll out a sheet at setting No.6 on the pasta machine, texture with a sponge, and stamp out eight flowers. Texture the edges to soften them.

4 The final color to mix is Hemlock, a pale green/turquoise blend. For this color use ¼ block of Peacock Pearl, ¼ block of Jungle, and ½ block of White. Repeat the stamping out and texturing of the flower shapes as for Radiant Orchid.

5 Place all 16 flowers on polyester batting and slightly curl the petals of four of each color to give a more natural look. Bake the bangle, flowers, and filled spacers according to the clay manufacturer's instructions.

6 Mix a quantity of two-part epoxy resin. Put a dot of the glue between the pairs of a flat and curled petal flowers, offsetting the petals. Press together, add another tiny dot to the middle, and press on the spacer beads. Leave until all layers are stuck together then mix a tiny amount of epoxy resin and attach the flowers to the bangle.

Always use a strong glue such as two-part epoxy resin to attach polymer clay to metal.

Earrings

YOU WILL NEED

Leftover clay from main project

Needle tool

2 x 2mm silver-colored beads

2 x silver-colored earwires

2 x 6mm jumprings

Make two flowers, following the steps for the main project. Use a smaller cutter so the flowers are a suitable size for earrings. Make a tiny hole in each flower with the needle tool. Add a silver bead to the center of each flower and bake. When cool, attach the flowers to earwires using jumprings (see page 20).

Rainbow Blend

Using pearlized clays, Alison Gallant creates bright and cheerful flowers with just a hint of sparkle. The blend of colors in this pretty jewelry set creates a multi-tone rainbow effect.

FOR THE PENDANT YOU WILL NEED

⅛ block Premo! Sculpey Cadmium Yellow Hue (5572)

⅛ block Premo! Sculpey III Pearl (1101)

½ block Premo! Sculpey III Blue Pearl (1008)

¼ block Premo! Sculpey Accents Bright Green Pearl (5035)

¼ block Premo! Sculpey Red Pearl (1223)

½ block Premo! Sculpey White (5001)

½ block Premo! Sculpey Accents Translucent (5310)

Pasta machine

Tissue blade or craft knife

Ruler

Round cutters in 1½in (37mm) and ⅜in (1cm)

Craft roller

Old credit card

Sheet of plastic wrap

Wet/dry sandpaper

Coarse cloth such as denim

3ft (1m) faux suede

Pendant

1 Mix the Cadmium Yellow and Pearl blocks together. Condition the clay using ¼ block each of blue, green, and red pearl clays on setting No.1 of the pasta machine (see page 16). Form all four colors into rectangles about 1½in (38mm) wide and 6in (150mm) long, slightly overlap the sheets so that the width of the four stripes fit into your pasta machine. Make an overlay blend (see page 18); roll through the pasta machine around 20 times. Fold in half the matching colors, turn 90 degrees and roll through to make a rainbow sheet about 10in (250mm) long and 2¾in (70mm) wide.

2 Condition the White and Translucent clays. Form each into a sheet about 2¾in (70mm) wide. Roll through a pasta machine starting at the thickest setting and reducing by one setting until the sheets are 11in (280mm) long. Lay the White on your work surface and trim the ends to make them straight. Place the rainbow blend on top, leaving about ⅜in (1cm) of White showing either end. Roll over the flat sheets gently with a craft roller to remove air bubbles. Trim the Translucent sheet slightly shorter than the rainbow blend and place on top. Repeat the rolling to remove air. Cut both ends at a 45-degree angle and roll up tightly.

3 Press an old credit card lengthways into the cane, almost to the center. Turn the cane 90 degrees and press down again. Repeat twice and then press between these indentations to make eight depressions in all. Your cane will now be distorted to give the look of a chrysanthemum flower.

4 Cut the cane in half to reduce one piece to about ⅝in (15mm) diameter (see page 17). Roll the remaining Blue Pearl through a pasta machine on the thickest setting, No.1. Cut thin slices from the cane and lay three on the Blue sheet overlapping them. Smooth them gently with your fingers, then roll to press them into the Blue. Lay the plastic wrap over the sheet and cut out the clay for the pieces you are making.

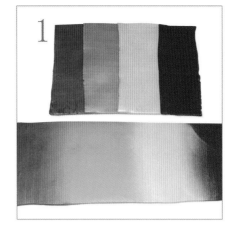

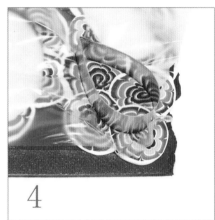

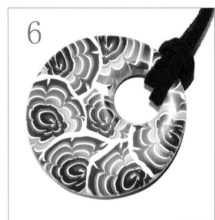

5 Remove the plastic wrap and cut out a small circle near the top of the pendant. Bake the pendant on the tile according to the clay manufacturer's instructions.

6 Finely sand using fine-grit paper and buff to a shine using coarse cloth or denim. Loop faux suede through the hole in the pendant and tie the ends.

Place a sheet of strong plastic wrap over the patterned clay sheet before cutting to give a softer edge. It also helps to remove any fingerprints.

Earrings

YOU WILL NEED

Scraps of polymer clay from the main project

Cane made in main project

Needle tool

2 x 5mm silver-colored jumprings

2 x silver-colored earwires

Make teardrop-shaped earrings in the same way as the pendant, but make a hole at the top of the teardrop with a needle tool. Bake and sand the pieces. Attach jumprings to the holes and add earwires before closing the rings (see page 20). Make sure that the patterned sides of the earrings face forward.

Bag charm

YOU WILL NEED

Scraps of polymer clay from the main project

Cane made in main project

2 x daisy spacer beads

1 x 2in (50mm) silver-colored headpin

1 x 5mm silver-colored jumpring

1 x silver-colored trigger clasp

Roll a ½in (12mm) ball of scrap clay and cover it with a thin layer of Blue Pearl left over from the main project. Cut thin slices of cane (made in the main project) and cover the ball, overlapping slices. Roll in your hands to smooth and form into a tube. Roll two small pieces of Blue Pearl into balls, flatten and repeat with tiny pieces of Bright Green Pearl. Press them onto each end of the tube. Pierce through the length with your needle tool, then bake. When cool, thread one daisy spacer onto the headpin, pass the pin through the bag charm, add another spacer bead, and turn a simple loop. Add a jumpring and clasp to complete (see page 20).

Either suspend round or tube clay beads on a wire, or embed in cornflour before baking to avoid flat or shiny marks on the surface.

Flower Set

For this gorgeous collection, Kay Vincent has taken inspiration from bright summer colors. Here she shows how to make this flowery jewelry, which you can adapt to match your summer clothes—great for a vacation!

FOR THE RING
YOU WILL NEED

⅓ block Premo! Sculpey White (5001)

1 block Premo! Sculpey Pomegranate (5026) or Purple (5513)

Pasta machine

Tissue blade or craft knife

Sheet of blank copy paper

1 x 7mm acrylic or glass cabochon bead

1 x ring blank

Two-part epoxy resin

Ring

1 Condition the clay by rolling both colors through the pasta machine at setting No.1 (see page 16) or roll each color into a ball by hand and then into a snake five times. Roll the White clay into a cylinder about 2in (50mm) long. Roll the Pomegranate into a long, thin sheet and wrap it around the cylinder. Roll out the cylinder until it is a cane, about 6in (150mm) long.

2 Cut off two sides of the cane so that the White is just starting to show through the Pomegranate. Reduce the cane until it is about 200mm (8in) long. Start at one end of the cane and press both sides inward, gradually working along the cane until it is longer and thinner. You can also try stretching the cane from both ends to lengthen it.

3 Cut the cane in half and squeeze the two pieces flat against each other to create a cane with two stripes. As in the previous step, reduce the cane until it is about 200mm (8in) long. To keep the rectangular shape you can occasionally flip the cane 90 degrees, so that a different edge rests against the flat surface.

4 Repeat Step 3 another six times (so that there are 4 white stripes, then 8, then 16, 32, 64, and 128). It is better to gradually lengthen the cane than to try to stretch it all in one go. Occasionally flip it 90 degrees so that a different edge is now on the flat surface. Cut off the ends of the cane if they become too distorted.

5 To reduce the width of the cane to ⅜in (10mm), start from one end and work along the cane, gently squeezing the sides together. Flip the cane 180 degrees so that the top edge is now on the flat surface, and repeat the squeezing process. If it starts to get too tall, squeeze from the top and bottom sides as well.

6 Again, working from one end of the cane to the other, firmly pinch the top edges together to create a point. The angle of the point will determine the number of petals that your flower has. If the angle is about 72 degrees this will result in a five-petal flower; if it is 60 degrees you will end up with a six-petal flower, and so on.

7 Hold the upper point of the triangle between your thumb and forefinger, and with your other thumb and forefinger press the lower triangle points inward so that they become more rounded. Work your way along the cane using the same action.

8 Cut slices from the cane about ⅛in (2mm) thick and arrange them into a flower shape. Press the clay onto a sheet of of blank copy paper, ensuring that the petals fuse together. Bake the piece (still on the paper) according to the clay manufacturer's instructions.

9 Glue the cabochon to the flower using two-part epoxy resin. Once it has set, glue the flower to the ring blank.

Avoid using superglues with acrylic cabochons, as the glue often reacts with the acrylic and spoils their appearance.

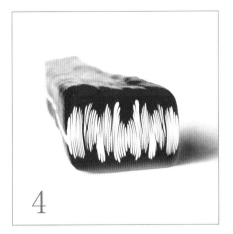

4

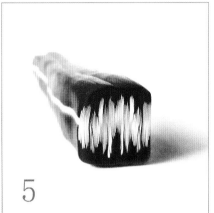

5

6

7

8

9

Earrings

YOU WILL NEED

Flower cane from
the main project

2 x flat pad ear posts

2 x 2mm acrylic gems

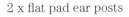

Reduce or stretch the cane (see page 17) to make
smaller flower petals. Follow the steps for the main
project to make up a flower shape for each earring,
then bake. When cool, glue the mini flowers to earring
stud backs using two-part epoxy resin and glue a tiny
gem to the center of each.

Brooch

YOU WILL NEED

Flower cane from the main project

1 x brooch bar

1 x 7mm acrylic or glass cabochon bead

Make a flower following the steps for the main project.
Simply glue a brooch bar to the piece instead of a
ring blank when you get to Step 9. Decorate with the
cabochon, and secure in place
with two-part epoxy resin.

Stunning Spirals

Kay Vincent has utilized swirls of color for this lovely set, which creates a striking spiral pattern. Beautiful in bright or muted colors, you can make them to match a specific outift or simply to complement the season.

FOR THE BRACELET YOU WILL NEED

1½ blocks Premo! Sculpey White (5001)

½ block of Premo! Sculpey Cobalt Blue (5063)

Pasta machine

Tissue blade or craft knife

Needle tool

10 x 2in (50mm) silver-colored eyepins

5 x 8mm faceted glass beads

2 x large (7mm) silver-colored jumprings

1 x lobster clasp

Wire cutters

Round-nose pliers

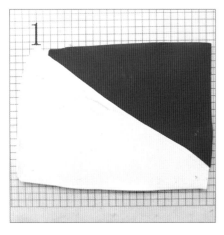

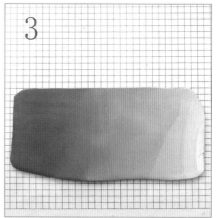

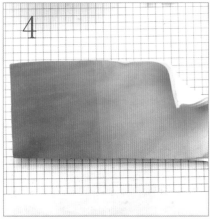

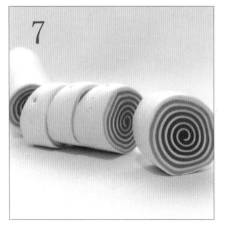

Bracelet

1   Condition the clay (see page 16). Roll each color through the pasta machine. Using half a block of White and half a block of Cobalt Blue clay, roll out a sheet of each color on the pasta machine at setting No.1. Trim the sheets into triangles and arrange them as a rectangle about 5in (120mm) wide.

2   To create a Skinner blend (see page 19), fold the sheet in half so that the top edge touches the bottom edge. Always start rolling from the folded edge first to prevent bubbles forming in the clay.

3   Repeat Step 2 up to 25 times, or until the sheet is thoroughly blended (it should be light at one end and dark at the other end). The sheet should always be folded in the same way (top to bottom), so keep note of which edge of the sheet was last to come out of the pasta machine. This top edge should then be folded over to touch the bottom edge.

4   Roll out the remainder of the White clay into a sheet about ⅛in (2mm) thick. Stack it on top of the blue/white sheet and trim the edges of the sheets to obtain a neat rectangle.

5   Roll this two-layered sheet to about ⅛in (2mm) thick, starting from the dark end of the sheet. This will create a longer sheet so that it can be rolled into the spiral pattern.

6   Start rolling the sheet from the darker edge, so that a spiral pattern is created, then carefully roll the cane until it is about ⅜in (10mm) in diameter. Let the cane rest for at least ten minutes so that it cools down and becomes firmer.

7   Slice the cane into widths of about ¼in (7mm) thick, and use a needle tool to create a hole through the side of each bead. The number of beads for the bracelet depends on the size of your wrist, but aim to make at least ten. Bake according to the clay manufacturer's instructions.

8   Take an eyepin and slide a bead onto it. Cut the wire end off about ⅜in (10mm) away from the bead and make a loop (see page 21). Repeat this step with all the faceted beads and five polymer clay discs.

9   Link the loops so that they form a bracelet, alternating the beads and polymer discs (the number of links depends on the size of your wrist.) Add a large jumpring (see page 20) to each end of the bracelet, and attach a clasp to one end.

Earrings

YOU WILL NEED

Scraps of polymer clay

Cane from the main project

4 x blue size 6 seed beads

4 x 6mm silver-colored spacer beads

2 x 2in (50mm) silver-colored headpins

2 x silver-colored earwires

Roll out a thin cylinder of scrap clay about ¼in (6mm) diameter and 2½in (60mm) long. Cut very thin slices from the end of the spiral cane and cover the cylinder with the slices. Cut two pieces from the cylinder that are about 1in (25mm) long and use a needle tool to make holes down the center, then bake. When cool, thread a seed bead, spacer, the polymer cylinder, spacer then another seed bead onto a headpin. Make a simple loop at the top and add an earwire before closing the loop (see page 21).

Keyring or charm

YOU WILL NEED

Scrap of polymer clay

Cookie cutter

Cane from the main project

1 x gold-colored keyring finding

1 x 8mm gold-colored jumpring

Cut out a shape (such as a heart) from scrap clay using a small cookie cutter. Cut very thin slices from the end of the spiral cane and apply these to one side of the heart. Use a needle tool to make a hole at the top of the heart. Bake the piece then cover the other side with spirals and bake again. When cool, add a keyring finding to the hole with an 8mm jumpring (see page 20).

Retro Chic

This fabulous set by Alison Gallant is a bright and dynamic mix of bold patterns. The colors zing out, ensuring you stand out from the crowd.

FOR THE NECKLACE YOU WILL NEED

½ block Premo! Sculpey Peacock Pearl (5038)

½ block Premo! Sculpey Pearl (5101)

½ block Premo! Sculpey Fuchsia (5504)

½ block Premo! Sculpey Pomegranate (5026)

½ block Premo! Sculpey Wasabi (5022)

1 Block Premo! Sculpey White (5001)

Pasta machine

Tissue blade or craft knife

Tile

2 x round cutters: 1⅜in (35mm) and 1⅛in (29mm)

Wet/dry sandpaper

Coarse cloth such as denim

Sheet of blank copy paper

Pin vise and 1.5mm drill bit

10 x 5mm jumprings

4 x 3mm jumprings

6ft (2m) faux suede or ribbon

Flat-nose pliers

Copy paper for smoothing surface

Necklace

1 Mix ½ block of Peacock Pearl with ¼ block of Pearl to lighten the color. Then mix ½ block each of Fuchsia and Pomegranate to make a cherry red shade. Condition ¼ block of Wasabi and ¾ block of White and prepare three offset Skinner blends (see page 19) using the same amount of the other two color mixes.

2 Roll each one through the pasta machine at setting No.1. Fold from bottom to top, until the sheets are blended across. Turn them 90 degrees and roll through twice more, color first, reducing the thickness by two numbers each time. Roll up tightly from white to color. Reduce to about ³⁄₈in (10mm) diameter and cut into three.

3 To make an ikat cane, stack the logs as shown, turn on its point and squash straight down with your fingers. Roll through the pasta machine at setting No.1. Cut in half, stack, offsetting the slices and repeat three times, keeping the pattern consistent. Carefully form into a circle, about 1¹³⁄₁₆in (45mm). Cut a slice and place on a tile for baking.

4 Using the colors and white, make three bullseye canes. Start with a log, diameter ³⁄₁₆in (5mm) or less and about 1⅛in (29mm) long, from cherry red mix, Wasabi, and Peacock Pearl mix. Wrap in White and add a final wrap of color other than cherry red. Vary the thicknesses of wrapping, cut a small piece off each log, and reduce (see page 17) it to give two sizes in each colorway.

5 Roll a sheet about 3¼in x 1⁹⁄₁₆in (80 x 40mm) of cherry red at setting No.2 or No.3 on the pasta machine. Place on a tile and cut thin slices from the bullseye canes and position them randomly on the sheet. After every five or six slices, cover with paper and roll gently with your fingertips to incorporate into the sheet. When you like the result, stamp out two circles of 1⅜in (35mm) diameter. Leave flat or place on a domed surface if you prefer a domed shape.

Ring

YOU WILL NEED

Section of ikat cane from main project (see Step 3)

Small piece of scrap clay

1 x ring blank

Reduce a piece of the ikat cane (see page 17). Place a small amount of flattened scrap clay in the center of a square or round ring blank and place the cane slice on top. Bake, sand, and buff as in the main project.

6 Roll a sheet about 2¾in x 1⅜in (70 x 35mm) of cherry red and place it on paper. Using the remainder of the three colors, roll small sheets slightly wider than 2¾in (70mm) through setting No.4 or No.5 on the pasta machine. Cut strips from each, varying the width and place on a base sheet. When full, cover with paper and gently press strips together to join seams. Stamp out two circles of 1⅛in (29mm) diameter.

7 Bake according to the manufacturer's instructions. Sand the tops using fine sandpaper. If the beads are domed, sand the bottom edges to reduce the thickness slightly and then the inside of the domes. If flat, sand the backs the same as the fronts, then buff to a shine using coarse cloth or denim.

8 Lay out the beads in order. With the pin vise, carefully drill holes either side of each bead. Insert jumprings in each hole (see page 20) and use another one to link the pairs except for the extreme left and right.

9 Cut the faux suede or ribbon in two, loop through the rings attached to the smallest beads and tie at your preferred length. If you prefer to add a clasp, measure the cord to the right length then add a ribbon crimp and a clasp.

Earrings

YOU WILL NEED

Section of bullseye canes (see Step 4 of main project)

Small piece of cherry red polymer clay

2 x silver-colored earwires

2 x 5mm jumprings

Make another sheet of bullseye cane slices following Step 5 of the main project. Stamp out two medium circles and place inside domes (like a cake tray for making cake pops) to make concave pieces. Bake. When cool, sand and buff the earrings. Drill holes in the domes then add jumprings and attach the earwires before closing the jumprings (see page 20).

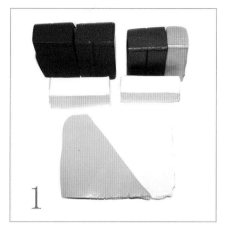

1

2

3

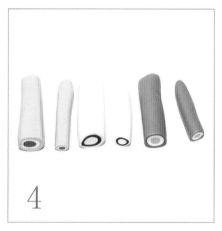

4

5

6

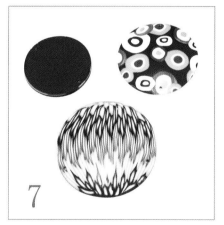

7

8

9

Always use the same brand of clay in
one project as they all have different
baking temperatures.

Summer Squiggles

Debbie Bulford shows how to create fabulous polymer clay jewelry in zingy shades of orange, lime, and plum. Combine the attractive beads with stunning red aventurine and amethyst gemstones.

FOR THE NECKLACE YOU WILL NEED

½ block Premo! Sculpey Orange (5033)

½ block Premo! Sculpey Wasabi (5022)

½ block Premo! Sculpey III Blue Pearl (1008)

½ block Premo! Sculpey Green (5323)

½ block Premo! Sculpey Cadmium Yellow Hue (5572)

½ block Premo! Sculpey Candy Pink (5523)

½ block Premo! Sculpey Purple (5513)

½ block Premo! Sculpey Gold (1086)

½ block Premo! Sculpey Ecru (5093) or Black (5042)

Pasta machine

⁹⁄₁₆in (14mm) round cutter

Cocktail stick

Tissue blade or craft knife

Coarse wet/dry sandpaper

Metal pins for baking

Clay extruder

9 x 10mm amethyst faceted beads

8 x 8mm red aventurine rondelles

1 x 25mm toggle clasp

2 x silver-colored crimp beads

1 x roll of nylon-coated beading wire

Chain-nose pliers

Side cutters

Bracelet

YOU WILL NEED

Scraps of Premo! Sculpey colors from main project

Elastic cord

Texture sheet (optional)

12 x amethyst faceted wheel

12 x red aventurine rondelles

5 x silver-colored ball-ended headpins

5 x 3mm silver-colored beads

1 x 6mm silver-colored jumpring

Make polymer discs following the main project instructions. A texture sheet could be used to texture the surface of the discs instead of sandpaper. Take the elastic cord and thread the discs on with the amethyst wheels and aventurine rondelles spaced between (keep five for the headpins). When the bracelet is the right length to fit around your wrist add the jumpring and tie a double knot to secure. Make up headpins with the five spare beads placing one bead and then the 3mm silver bead on a headpin and making a simple loop (see page 21). Attach all these pieces to the jumpring on the bracelet.

Necklace

1 Choose four main colors and mix a portion of them with a small amount of Ecru or Black clay to give a variety of shades for your spacer discs. To make uniform-sized beads, use the four main colors and pass through your pasta machine on setting No.1 (see page 16). Use a round cutter to cut out 18 circles and roll into beads.

2 Feed the remaining colors through the pasta machine on setting No.1. Fold over all the sheets of clay to make a double layer and cut 30 rounds with a ⁹⁄₁₆in (14mm) cutter. Use a cocktail stick to make a hole in the center.

3 Lift each disc using your tissue blade or craft knife and place between two pieces of coarse sandpaper and press together. Feed onto a metal pin and prepare to bake.

4 To make the strings, roll 10 pea-sized rounds using the leftover clay from Step 2. The extruder comes with a selection of cutters; use the smallest single hole. Place one of the rounds into the barrel and turn the handle. Repeat for each one.

5 Make a hole in one of the beads, pick up a string and loop it onto your bead. Thread your completed beads onto pins. Bake according to the clay manufacturer's instructions.

6 Working on the roll of beading wire, thread on all the polymer clay beads and gemstones in a random pattern. When you have achieved your desired necklace length add a crimp bead to the end and then one half of the toggle clasp. Feed the wire back through the crimp bead and pull to create a small loop with the clasp attached. Squash the crimp closed with chain-nose pliers and cut off any excess wire. Push all the beads up to the end and cut beading wire about 2in (50mm) away from the last bead, add a crimp bead and the other part of the toggle clasp. Repeat the instructions to create a loop, close the crimp and cut off excess wire.

Roll the beads slowly between the palms of your hands using tiny movements to make an even, round bead.

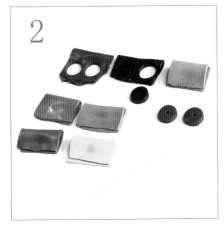

Earrings

YOU WILL NEED

Polymer clay in two colors

2 x silver-colored ball-ended headpins

2 x silver-colored earwires

Chain-nose pliers

Make up two squiggle ball beads following the main steps, bake and then thread them onto headpins. Make a simple loop (see page 21) at the top and attach them to earwires. Twist the loop gently to the side with chain-nose pliers and thread on the earwire then close the loop (see page 20).

Clay extruders are very versatile and come with a wide range of shaped discs for fun extrusions.

Red Skies

Nina Fletcher has created this wonderful collection, including a very unusual chain-linked necklace, using soft and fiery sunset colors.

FOR THE NECKLACE YOU WILL NEED

1 block Premo! Sculpey Orange (5033)

½ block Premo! Sculpey Ecru (5093)

¼ block Premo! Sculpey Denim (5003)

¼ block Premo! Sculpey Black (5042)

⅛ block Premo! Sculpey Cadmium Red Hue (5382)

Pasta machine

Found objects for texturing

2 x round cutters 1³⁄₁₆in (30mm) and 1⅜in (35mm)

Tissue blade or craft knife

Gilder's paste or acrylic/oil paint and brushes

Gloves (optional)

Old rags/kitchen towel

Clasp (with jumpring attached)

Two-part epoxy resin

2 x 48in (122cm) x ¹⁄₃₂in (1mm) colored cord

12in (300mm) approx. scrap wire (any fine gauge)

Side cutters

KEY:
Ecru (1),
Orange (2),
Denim (3),
Cadmium Red Hue (4),
Black (5)

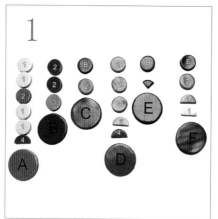

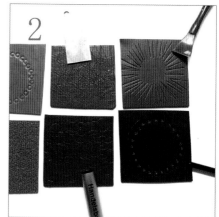

Bracelet

YOU WILL NEED

Black polymer clay

Scraps of polymer clay from main project

Needle tool

Elastic cord

7 x 6mm black beads

Make round black clay beads and roll the scraps from the main project into the surface. Roll them in your hands to smooth and shape. Pierce with a needle tool and bake. When cool, string onto elastic cord with a small black bead in between and tie a double knot to secure.

The inner diameter of the links in this necklace should be more than twice the width of the rings, otherwise the links will not fit together.

Necklace

1 Mix the six colors A–F shown in the image by following the color and quantity guide. As colors will be used in pairs for each link of the necklace you should aim to have the same quantity of each color. Roll the clay through a pasta machine at setting No.3 (see page 16).

2 After rolling the clays, roughly cut out the shapes. Choose your texturing tool. You could use found items, such as bits from an old ballpoint pen, sandpaper, or the end of a paintbrush. Make a faint mark with your two cutters on the clay before texturing; it will be easier to center the texture. Decide on which colors will be paired, or you could make each chain link a separate color.

3 Place both textured layers of clay on top of each other. It will be easier lining the cutter up if there is only one side textured with the small circles. Make sure this layer is facing up. Take the larger cutter and cut out the circle. Remove any excess clay. Align the smaller cutter on the clay, carefully center it, and cut. Remove the excess clay.

4 Once all the chain links have been cut out, place them on a tile. Use a template to achieve the desired shapes. Draw the shapes (circles, ovals, or random organic shapes) on a sheet of paper and place the links on top. Bake according to the clay manufacturer's instructions. The cutting of the links will be done once the links are baked to avoid drag and distortion in the clay.

5 Once the links are cool, paint them with Gilder's paste. Oils or acrylic paints can also be used. It may be useful to wear gloves. Take care not to paint the inside or the outside of the links if you only want the face of the links to be embellished with the paint. Once the paste/paint has dried a little bit, rub off the excess with old rags or kitchen towel.

6 Make two small cylinders in polymer clay to match the chain. Take a piece of cord, fold in half, and then in half again. Thread on a chain link, and bring the cord ends together. Gently pull one loop about ½in (13mm) above the ends. Wrap the cord ends in scrap wire until they hold together. You should end up with four strands of cord around the polymer clay link. Take some scrap clay and cover the wire ends, form into a bead shape, and make sure all the wire is hidden and the longer loop is showing above the clay bead. Now bake all the chain links and the cord sections. Allow to cool then take a tissue blade or craft knife and cut half of the chain links at an angle. Assemble the chain by gently opening the cut links and sliding on the others to create a chain. Add the links with cord attached to the ends. Glue all the cuts back together with two-part epoxy. Attach the clasp to one end with the jumpring (see page 20).

If the clay feels sticky, leach it by placing it between sheets of blank copy paper with a weight on the top for an hour or longer.

Earrings

YOU WILL NEED

Scraps of polymer clay from main project

Black polymer clay

Pin vise and 1.5mm drill bit

2 x 6mm jumprings

2 x silver-colored earwires

Roll out Black clay on a pasta machine at setting No.4. Roll the colored scraps from chain links through the pasta machine at the same setting. Cut ultra-narrow strips of the scrap clay sheet and place them at random on Black clay. Lay paper over the sheet and rub gently with your finger to push the strips into the Black clay. Cut out rings (as in the main project) of patterned clay and smaller rings from the Black textured clay. Make oval pieces using the main project instructions then pinch the top of each oval to make it into a teardrop. Bake and when cool drill holes using a 1.5mm drill bit and a pin vise in the narrow end, then thread jumprings through the holes and earwires before closing the jumprings (see page 20).

Marvellous Mosaics

Chris Pellow loves Antonio Gaudí's work, and in particular his magnificent mosaics in Park Güell in Barcelona, Spain. The ceiling of the hall of columns with its amazing mosaics was the inspiration behind this set.

FOR THE NECKLACE YOU WILL NEED

1 x block Fimo Pearl

1 x block Fimo White

Scrap of Fimo Brown

Tissue blade or craft knife

Pasta machine

Sheet of plastic wrap

Craft roller

Round cutters in three sizes: ⅝in (15mm), ¾in (18mm), 1in (25mm)

Domed baking tray

Wet/dry sandpaper

Texture plate

Coarse cloth such as denim

Pin vise and 1.5mm drill bit

1 x roll of nylon-coated beading wire

2 x 12mm turquoise beads

4 x 10mm turquoise beads

10g x size 11 (1.8mm) red seed beads

4 x 6mm coral spacer beads

1 x clasp

2 x jumprings

6 x crimp beads

Side cutters

Chain-nose pliers

Earrings

YOU WILL NEED

Crackle clay sheet from Step 3 of the main project

2 x 4mm turquoise beads

10 x size 11 (1.8mm) red seed beads

2 x silver-colored headpins

2 x silver-colored earwires

Coarse cloth such as denim

Cut out four small circles from the patterned sheet and bake on the rounded surface as per Step 4 of the main project. Gently sand the bottom flat. Put a thin layer of liquid clay on the flat sides and push two circles together. Bake, sand, and buff one side to a shine. Drill as in Step 6 of the main project through the length of the beads. Take a headpin and place in this order: a red seed bead, turquoise bead, red seed bead, clay bead, 3 x red seed beads. Make a simple loop at the top (see page 21) and attach the earwire. Open the loop on the earwire by twisting the loop to one side (do not pull it outward) and thread onto the headpin. Close the loop by twisting it back in line with the earwire.

Necklace

1 Condition all the clay. You will need only a tiny bit of Brown clay to mix thoroughly with the Pearl clay to make a slightly darker sheet. Roll the clay through the pasta machine at setting No.3 (see page 16).

2 Roll the White clay into a big log. Stand it up. Cut from the top to the bottom. Place a piece of the darker layer on the cut surface and put the log back together. Repeat, cutting and replacing until you obtain a cane. Try to mimic a mosaic by cutting triangles and irregular shapes. Reduce the cane (see page 17), cut into several logs, and reassemble into one cane.

3 Roll a layer of scrap clay through the pasta machine at setting No.3. Cover with evenly sliced pieces from the mosaic cane and put them next to each other on the sheet. Cover with plastic wrap and gently roll with the craft roller to even out the cane slices and flatten the surface to make a crackle clay sheet. When you are happy with the result, cut out five circles: one large, two medium, and two smaller ones.

4 Place the circles on a rounded baking shape, such as paint mixing wells. Bake according to the clay manufacturer's instructions. Once cool, sand with rough sandpaper until the base is flat. This will assure a snug fit with the underside of the bead. Roll out the remainder Pearl clay through the pasta machine at setting No.3.

5 Place each bead with the sanded side onto the clay sheet and push them down slightly. Place the cutter over the clay/bead sandwich and cut out the circle. Use a tissue blade or craft knife to lift this part from the surface. Texture the base of the bead and cut away the protruding parts; a subtle texture from a leather couch sample has been used here. Bake the beads according to the clay manufacturer's instructions.

6 Sand the sides of the beads to get rid of any unsightly bits. Sand and buff the large and smaller beads to a high shine using coarse cloth or denim. Gently drill the holes in the hollow beads. To do this, use a pin vise and drill bit; place the bit in the vise and place the end of the drill bit where you want the hole to be, turn the pin vise clockwise pushing gently against the bead. You will feel it when you have drilled through to the hollow middle. Pull the bit out and turn the bead to drill in from the other side; repeat for all the beads. Drill the hole slightly above the center of the bead so the beads will drape nicely.

To put the necklace together, refer to the main image on page 78. Cut three pieces of beading wire, approx. 18in (460mm) long, and string the largest mosaic bead on all three; add the following on each side: coral spacer, 12mm turquoise bead, coral spacer, middle sized mosaic bead, red seed bead, 10mm turquoise, red seed bead, small mosaic, red seed bead, 10mm turquoise. Now separate the three strands and thread on as many red seed beads as you need to make the necklace a nice length. Stop when the length is right and make sure all three strands are the same length. Repeat for the other side of the necklace so the sides are level. Thread a crimp bead on the end of one strand, push the wire back through the crimp so a small loop is left in the end and squeeze closed with the chain-nose pliers. Repeat for all six strands. Open a jumpring (see page 20) and thread the loops on three strands (on one side) onto the jumpring. Close the ring. Repeat for the other side but add the clasp before you close the ring.

You can mix colors; for example, by using a tiny speck of Black mixed with the Pearl clay to obtain a gray sheet.

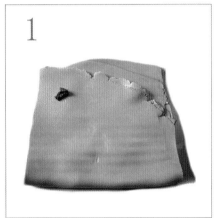

1

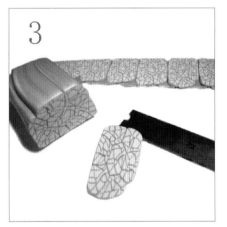

2

3

4

5

6

Make a much wider necklace with tapering end pieces to the width of the clasp for an alternative look.

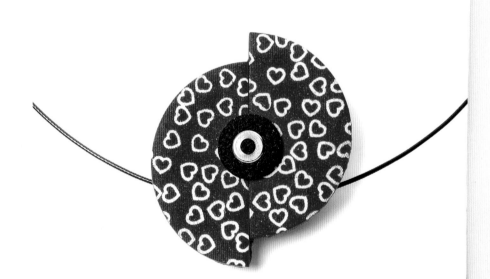

Hearts in the Round

This classic vintage style design by Alison Gallant is reminiscent of romantic Art Deco shapes with modern confetti hearts. Simple to make and easy to adapt, this quirky little set will complement any outfit.

FOR THE NECKLACE YOU WILL NEED

1 block Premo! Sculpey Pomegranate (5026)

Small piece Premo! Sculpey Accents Pearl (5101)

Small piece Premo! Sculpey Black (5042)

Pasta machine

Silk screen

Tube of white acrylic paint

Squeegee (or old credit card)

Paper towel

Liquid polymer clay

Wet/dry sandpaper

Sponge or coarse sandpaper

3 x round cutters: ⁹⁄₁₆in (14mm), ⁵⁄₈in (16mm) and 1¾in (45mm)

1 x silver-colored washer

Tissue blade or craft knife

1 x steel cable wire choker

Two-part epoxy resin

1 x magnet clasp

Sheet of paper

Work quickly when spreading the paint over the screen to stop the paint drying, but be sure it is dry before cutting it.

1

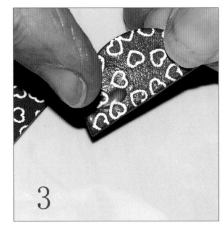

2

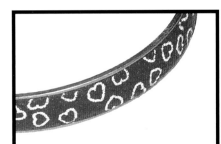

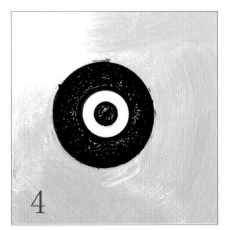

3

4

Bangle

YOU WILL NEED

Scraps from the silk-screen sheet

1 x channel bangle blank

Cut narrow slices of clay from the sheet and place in the channel of the bangle. Texture with a sponge and bake. Add liquid polymer clay to seal the surface, paint, and bake again.

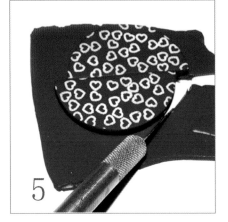

5

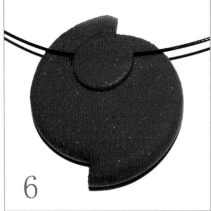

6

If you don't have silk screens, try pushing in some impression plates, or painting on your hearts with acrylic paints or pen and ink.

Pendant

1 Condition and mix the Pomegranate and Pearl clays. Roll the sheets through the pasta machine at setting No.1 (see page 16). Lay the silk screen on the clay, shiny side down, and smooth to remove any air. Squeeze white paint along a short edge, with your squeegee at a 45-degree angle. Pull the squeegee toward you, pushing the paint through the screen.

2 Carefully lift one corner to see if the paint has transferred successfully. If there are gaps, let the screen drop back onto the clay and repeat. Remove the screen and wash immediately under cold running water. With shiny side up, leave to dry on a paper towel.

3 When the paint is dry, stamp out a 1¹³/₁₆in (45mm) circle and cut it across the middle. Keep the remainder of the sheet for extra projects. Bake both halves of the circle, remove from the oven and, while still warm, wipe a thin layer of liquid polymer clay over the surfaces and bake again for 10 minutes. This seals the paint.

4 Lightly sand the flat and curved edges with very fine sandpaper. Mix a tiny piece of Black clay with a pinch of Pearl. Roll through the pasta machine at setting No.4, texture with a sponge or coarse sandpaper, and stamp out a ⁹/₁₆in (14mm) circle. Press a silver-colored washer into the clay and bake.

5 Roll the Pomegranate clay through the pasta machine at setting No.3 and place on the paper. Smear a little liquid polymer clay between the middle cut and on the backs of the two silk-screened halves. Slightly offset them and press together onto the Pomegranate clay. Cut round with a tissue blade or craft knife, turn over on the paper and texture the back and all of the joins.

6 Roll a tiny piece of Pomegranate clay through the pasta machine at setting No.1. Texture, then stamp out a ⁵/₈in (16mm) circle. Press the wire choker into the back of the clay to form a channel. Bake according to the clay manufacturer's instructions. Mix a little two-part epoxy resin. Attach the Black clay and silver washer to the front of the pendant and the Pomegranate channel piece onto the back. Thread the wire through the channel and stick into the magnet clasp.

When silk screening, make sure the clay will not shift when applying the paint.

Earrings

YOU WILL NEED

Scraps from the silk-screen sheet

Pin vise and 0.8mm drill bit

4in (100mm) x US 20 gauge (SWG21, 0.8mm) silver-colored wire

Side cutters

Superglue

2 x silver-colored spacers

2 x 4mm black pearls

2 x silver-colored earwires

Chain- or flat-nose pliers

Stamp out a 1³/₁₆in (30mm) circle from a silk-screen sheet, cut in half, and bake. While still warm, wipe a thin layer of liquid polymer clay over the surfaces and bake again for 10 minutes to seal the paint. Add a textured back using the instructions from Step 4 of the main project and bake for a third time. With a pin vise and a 0.8mm drill bit, drill a hole in the clay semicircles about ¼in (6mm) from the straight side. Take the wire and cut in half with side cutters. Push the wire into the hole made in the semicircles and add a little superglue to secure it. Thread on a spacer and pearl then make a simple loop at the top (see page 21). Attach to earwires using chain- or flat-nose pliers. Open the loop on the earwire by twisting the loop to one side (do not pull it outward) and thread on the earring piece. Close the loop by twisting it back in line with the earwire (see page 20).

Flaming Hot

This bold collection by Alison Gallant uses the warm, fiery colors of reds, oranges, and yellows and its vibrancy makes a strong impact on any outfit.

FOR THE NECKLACE YOU WILL NEED

¾ block Premo! Sculpey Pomegranate (5026)

¼ block Premo! Sculpey Cadmium Yellow Hue (5572)

¼ block Premo! Sculpey Orange (5033)

¾ block Premo! Sculpey Black (5042)

Pasta machine

2 x sheets of gold leaf substitute

Ripple blade (a tissue blade with a wavy edge)

Ovenproof tile

Petal-shaped cutters in 1¹¹⁄₁₆in (43mm) and 1⅜in (35mm)

Piece of card stock

Sheet of blank copy paper

Polyester batting

Cyanoacrylate adhesive (superglue)

Needle tool

Wet/dry sandpaper

Coarse cloth such as denim

15in (380mm) length of beading thread

Chain-nose and round-nose pliers

2 x calottes

1 x medium lobster claw clasp

1 x 5mm jumpring

Pendant

YOU WILL NEED

Pattern clay sheet from main project

Ready-made leather thong necklace

Use the 1¹¹/₁₆in (43mm) cutter to stamp out a circle from the patterned sheet for a pendant. Cut a 10mm circle near the top. Bake, sand, and buff. Thread onto a leather thong necklace or cord.

Earrings

YOU WILL NEED

Pattern clay sheet from main project

2 x silver-colored earwires

2 x 8mm silver-colored jumprings

From the patterned sheet described in Step 6, cut two petal shapes to make earrings. Pierce small holes in the top of the petals with a needle tool before baking. Open the jumprings and attach a petal to each one, add an earwire before closing the jumprings (see page 20).

Necklace

1   Condition and roll the Pomegranate, Cadmium Yellow Hue, and Orange clays through the pasta machine at setting No.1 (see page 16). Form four sheets about 5½ x 2¾in (140 x 70mm), two in Pomegranate. The next stage uses gold leaf substitute, which is very thin, tears easily, and flies away if not treated with care.

2   Open the packet of leaf and lay the Cadmium Yellow Hue on the lower half of a sheet. Smooth to remove any air bubbles and fold the clay and leaf over to encase the yellow. Lay a sheet of Pomegranate on one side. Using a second gold-leaf sheet, repeat with Orange clay and the second piece of Pomegranate. Press together, cut in half, and stack.

3   Cut and stack again to give 16 layers of clay interleaved with gold. Take the ripple blade and cut down through all layers and across the stack at around ⅛in (3mm) intervals. Press together, turn 45 degrees, and repeat. Compress into a rough cube to help distort the layers. Leave to cool and firm up for a couple of hours.

4   Press the stack firmly onto a tile to secure it. Roll half a block of Black on the pasta machine at setting No.2 and carefully lay down on an ovenproof tile. Shave off about six thin pieces from the stack at an angle and lay them on the Black clay, leaving small gaps to allow the Black to show through.

5   Cover the shavings with a piece of the interleaving paper from the gold leaf and smooth with your fingertips until you can't see any seams. Continue to slice and add a few shavings and smooth in regularly. When the Black is covered, roll over the sheet from all angles, still using the paper as a barrier.

6   Cut seven large petal shapes from the sheet using the 1⅜in (35mm) cutter and leave them in position on the tile. Carefully remove the excess clay and set aside for extra projects. Bake the petals according to the clay manufacturer's instructions. When cool, use very fine sandpaper to sand, then buff to a shine using coarse cloth or denim.

7   Roll out a ¼ block of Pomegranate through the pasta machine at setting No.3 and lay on your tile. Stamp out 25 small petals using the 1¹/₁₆in (43mm) cutter. Reserve seven. Take the other petals, one at a time, and carefully fold over, leaving a gap at the fold and pressing the points together. Fold over the remaining seven petals and place a small piece of card between the points.

8   Bake the folded petals on paper or polyester batting and sand and buff when cool. Using superglue, put a tiny spot on the top back of a large petal and slide a red folded petal over it. Carefully press together and remove any excess glue. Repeat with the remaining petals. Roll 34 x ⅜in (10mm) balls of Black clay and pierce with a needle tool. Bake according to the clay manufacturer's instructions. Sand with superfine sandpaper. Buff to a shine using coarse cloth or denim.

9   Take the length of beading thread and slide on the beads, making sure the large petals are arranged in the middle. Adjust the number of black ball beads to make the necklace to your preferred length. Take a calotte and push the thread through the hole in the hinge between the cups and make a big knot in the thread. Add a little glue and use the chain-nose pliers to squeeze the cups on the calotte closed around the knot. Repeat for the other end. With round-nose pliers, roll the end on the calotte into a loop, adding the clasp before closing the loop. Repeat on the other side to attach the jumpring.

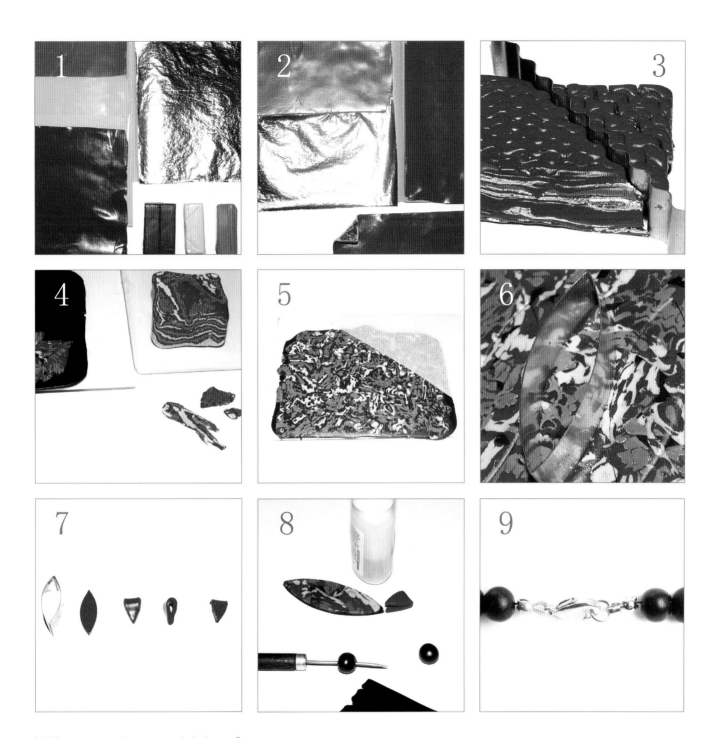

When using gold-leaf substitute, work slowly and away from any breeze.

Eastern Promise

This colorful set by Lizzi Holt is inspired by the hustle and bustle of vibrant spice markets. The extruded clay strings make a colorful impact. Use paler or softer-colored clay for a more subtle effect.

FOR THE NECKLACE YOU WILL NEED

½ block Premo! Sculpey Cadmium Yellow (5572)

½ block Premo! Sculpey Orange (5033)

½ block Premo! Sculpey Green (5323)

½ block Premo! Sculpey Purple (5513)

½ block Premo! Sculpey III Light Blue Pearl (1130)

½ block Premo! Sculpey Fuchsia (5504)

Small amount Premo! Sculpey Black (5042) or scrap clay

Pasta machine

1⅝in (40mm) round cutter

Small oven-safe round bowl

Tissue blade or craft knife

Clay extruder

Dishwashing liquid

Wet/dry sandpaper

Two-part epoxy resin

Varnish for a high shine finish (optional)

Blank copy paper and marker pen

Pin vise and 2mm drill bit

⅛in (2mm) hollow core black rubber cord

6 x O-rings

2 x 2mm round endcaps

1 x clasp

2 x 6mm jumprings

Necklace

1 Condition all the clays through the pasta machine at setting No.1. Roll out all the clays to about ¹⁄₃₂in (1mm) thick (see page 16). Cut out five circles— one in each of the colors using the 1⅝in (40mm) cutter. Gently lift and attach to the rounded outer surface of the round bowl. Lightly texture the circles with coarse sandpaper, taking care not to distort the shape too much. Bake according to the clay manufacturer's instructions. Remove from the bowl when cool and set aside. These will be the backs of your beads.

2 Roll out the Black or scrap clay and cut out another five circles and place them on the bowl as before. Make sure all the edges are firmly adhered to the bowl ready for the next stage. Do not texture or bake. These circles form the base for the front of your beads.

3 Take a small portion of each of the colored clays. Using a tissue blade or craft knife roughly chop and mix before squeezing together and rolling into a log. Assemble the extruder with a 12-hole cutter (¹⁄₃₂in/1mm holes). Extrude your multicolored log into strings. Untangle and set aside ready for use.

4 Take one of the strings and starting on the outer edge, press the end of the string onto the cut edge of a black circle and taper it a little with your finger. Continue around the edge and then keep going in a spiral fashion, adding extra strings as needed until you reach the center. Press the strings gently onto the Black clay and adjacent coils as you go.

5 Repeat the spirals on all the black circles, and then bake. Remove all the circles from the bowl when cool.

6 Add dishwashing liquid to a dishpan filled with 1in (25mm) of water. Place the sandpaper on the bottom and, holding the circles with dome side up, sand the inside edge of all the circles until the edges are tapered and flat. The dishwashing liquid stops the sandpaper from clogging.

Ring

YOU WILL NEED

Premo! Sculpey colors and Black or scrap clay from the main project

1 x ring blank with flat pad

Make a smaller disc using the main project instructions, but don't drill a hole through the middle. When baked and cooled, glue onto a ring blank with two-part epoxy resin.

7 Pair up the fronts and backs of the beads and test how well they fit together. Carefully apply two-part epoxy resin to the inner edge of one half of the bead. Press on to the other half and hold until secure. Once fully dry, varnish one or both sides of the bead if desired.

8 On a sheet of blank copy paper, draw around one of the beads, then draw a horizontal line just above the center. Use this line to mark the position of the holes with a marker pen on each side of the beads. Use a 2mm drill bit with a pin vise to make the holes at the same angle as the line on the paper.

9 Thread all the beads onto the rubber cord with an O-ring at the ends and between each bead. Cut the cord to length. Add endcaps, jumprings, and a clasp to finish off. Glue on the endcaps and attach the clasp to one end and a single jumpring to the other (see page 20).

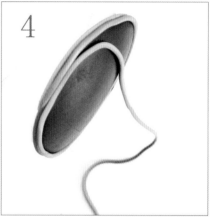

These discs would look great in graduating sizes!

Cufflinks

YOU WILL NEED

Premo! Sculpey colors and Black or scrap clay from the main project

2 x cufflink blanks with flat pad

Make two smaller discs using the main project instructions, but don't drill a hole through the middle. When baked and cooled, glue onto cufflink blanks with two-part epoxy resin.

Cool Blues

Make this cool retro set of designs created by Chris Pellow. Combine a simple technique with a few funky twists and turns to make stylish, matching pieces.

FOR THE PENDANT YOU WILL NEED

½ block Fimo in White

½ block Fimo in Turquoise

¾ block Fimo in Navy

½ block Fimo in Blue

Clay extruder

Tissue blade or craft knife

Acrylic roller

Metal ruler and knife (or cutters)

Disused toothbrush

Coffee cup (optional)

Snake chain

¾in (20mm) round cutter

Pendant

1 Condition all the clays through the pasta machine at setting No.1 (see page 16). Roll into flat sheets and cut out equal circles to fit in the extruder using the ¾in (20mm) round cutter. Combine White, Turquoise, Navy, and Blue—and repeat until you have a log three-quarters of the length of the extruder's barrel. Roll the log until it smoothly fits into the barrel. Add the disc with the square opening and the endcap. Start extruding by gently turning the handle.

2 Extrude the first cane by turning the handle until all the clay has been pushed out of the barrel. Cut the cane from the barrel. Wind the handle of the extruder all the way back and fill with another log. Repeat to obtain another cane. Discard the first and last ³⁄₁₆in (5mm) as these will be distorted and affect the combined cane. Divide each cane into 2in (50mm) long sections.

3 Closely align four cane sections, making sure to avoid any air gaps in between. Add another four on top. Alternate repeating patterns to give interest to the cane. Continue adding two more layers until a total of 16 canes form a combined retro cane. To reduce the cane, gently roll the block with a craft roller, turn it on its side, and repeat for all sides.

4 Roll out two small sheets of conditioned, even-colored Blue and Navy clay. Cut out a small and a larger square. These are homemade cutters which, unlike commercially available cookie cutters, have no visible seams because they are soldered together at the non-cutting side. You can just use a metal ruler and a knife, or any other shape if you prefer. You need the square to be approx. ¼in (6mm) bigger than the retro cane and the Blue square to be ¼in (6mm) bigger than the Navy one.

5 For this pendant, texture the smaller square with a disused toothbrush. You can also use an embossing pen or any other pin or stick to gently carve a pattern in the surface. Take care not to distort the edges of the square. Depending on your design choice, you can make the texture more intricate by using rubber stamps.

6 The retro cane has rested and firmed up, so it will now be easier to cut an even slice. Place the cane where you can look down onto it from above and position the blade to cut straight down. Gently push the blade through the cane (if making extra pieces, cut all the cane slices now).

7 Assemble the pendant by placing the retro cane slice onto the smaller Navy square, which is then stuck onto the larger blue one, either in the middle for a perfectly geometric design or offset for a variation. You can alternate textured sheets with even ones. Bake according to the clay manufacturer's instructions. You could try baking the pendant on a rounded surface (such as a coffee cup) for added interest.

8 From the sheet of Navy clay created in Step 4, cut a rectangle that is the same height at the Blue square and about one-third of the width.

9 Take the strip from Step 8 and position it halfway across the back of the pendant. Attach the top of the clay to the edge. Make an arch before attaching the bottom part of the strip. Allow enough space to accommodate the stringing material you want to use. For this pendant, snake chain has been used and initals added. Check the arch is large enough to take the chain then bake the pendant (without the chain) following the manufacturer's instructions.

4

5

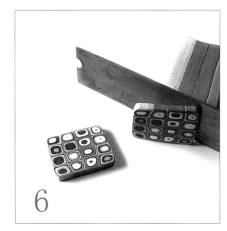

6

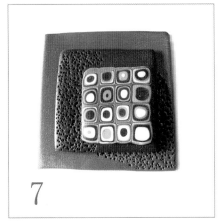

7

8

9

Cufflinks

YOU WILL NEED

Retro cane from the main project

Fimo in Navy

2 x cufflink blanks

Cut a thick slice from the retro cane, put the cufflink blank on top, and add a thin layer of Navy clay to the back, embedding the cufflink between the two layers of clay. Smooth and bake following the manufacturer's instructions.

Ring

YOU WILL NEED

Retro cane from the main project

Fimo in Navy

1 x ring blank with flat pad

Cut a thick slice from the retro cane, put the ring blank on top, and add a thin layer of Navy clay to the back, embedding the flat pad on the ring blank between the two layers of clay. Smooth and bake.

Add texture to a retro cane layer for a completely different but stylish look.

Try out different extruder disc shapes to obtain other effects.

Geometric Filigree

Emma Ralph shows you how to create a bold geometric set of stunning jewelry from multicolored strings. These striking pieces join together different patterns from extruded clay.

FOR THE PENDANT YOU WILL NEED

¼ block Cernit in Opaque White (029)

¼ block Cernit in Light-Green (019)

¼ block Cernit in Blue-Gray (016)

¼ block Cernit in Neon Light Fuchsia (922)

¼ block Cernit in Neon Light Yellow (700)

¼ block Cernit in Black (025)

Pasta machine

Clay extruder

Several small plain ceramic tiles

3 x 10mm antique copper jumprings

4 x 6mm antique copper jumprings

Square cutters (small and medium)

Alcohol ink (dark color)

Paintbrush

Sandpaper

Leather cord or chain

Chain-nose pliers

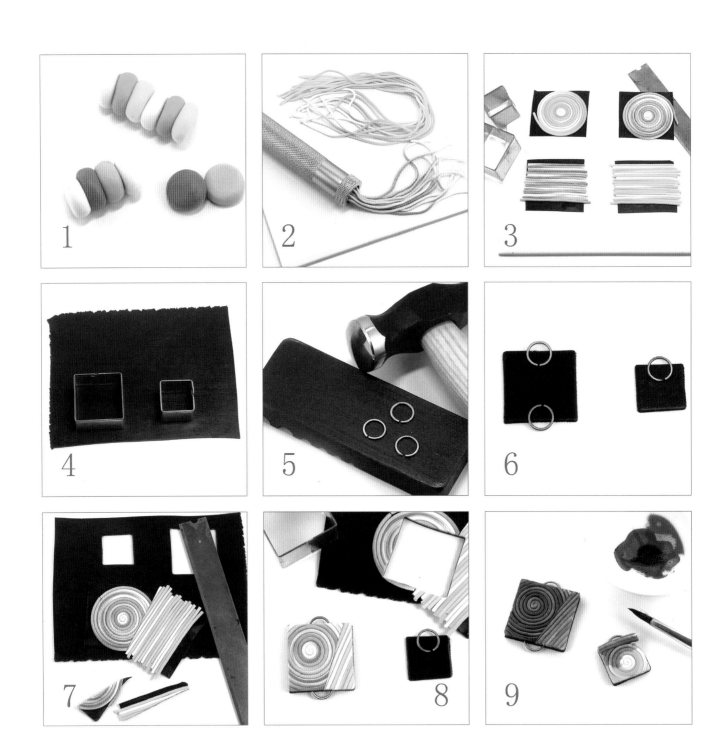

Vary the look with the size and shape of the clay strings. The extruder tools come with a multitude of discs for you to explore and other shapes are also available.

Necklace

1 Condition the clays through the pasta machine at setting No.1 (see page 16). Form four balls of Opaque White and two from the other colors, ⁹⁄₁₆in (14mm) in diameter. Flatten slightly. Starting with Opaque White, stack half the white and all the yellow and green pieces together, alternating the colors evenly. Form a separate stack using white, blue, and pink.

2 Load the yellow/green stack into the extruder barrel. Place the stack so the color nearest the screw-on cap is white. Fit the sieve die with ¹⁄₈in (2mm) perforations into the cap and attach to the barrel. Extrude the stack to form a pile of clay strings. Clean the extruder. Repeat for blue/pink.

3 Roll a Black sheet using the thinnest setting of the pasta machine and lay on a tile. Cut four sections a little larger than the biggest cutter. Arrange the strings on top to form spirals and linear patterns from each color. Gently push the clay down as you go. Slide a tissue blade under sections to remove from the tile.

4 Working on a fresh tile, lay out another Black clay sheet, this time rolled to a thickness of ¹⁄₃₂in (1mm). Make the sheet large enough to easily accommodate both cutters twice over—you won't need the entire sheet now, but the surplus will be used later. Cut out one large and one small square, leaving them in place on the tile. Remove the remaining clay sheet and set aside.

5 Take the 10mm and 6mm jumprings and hammer them on a steel surface to flatten and texture the edges.

6 To make the hanging loops, position the large jumprings on the clay squares so they overhang the edge. Place rings top and bottom on the large square and top only on the smaller one. Ensure each jumpring is centered and symmetrical and that the opening is on the clay side, not the overhang. When happy with the placement, push the jumprings down very slightly into the clay.

7 Lay the surplus Black clay sheet from Step 5 on a fresh tile. Take one of the spirals made earlier and cut away a small section with a tissue blade. Place the spiral on the sheet, pushing it down gently. Cut a slightly offset edge into the linear piece of the opposite color. Place it against the spiral, with the cut edges butted closely together, and push it down carefully.

8 Using the largest cutter, cut out a square and place it on top of the corresponding clay/jumpring base from Step 6. Take care not to disturb the jumprings or base and be sure to marry up the edges neatly. Push down softly to ensure all the parts are well connected. Using the remaining clay pieces, repeat the above steps and make the top for the smaller square base.

9 Bake both parts on the tile, following the clay manufacturer's instructions. Once cool, remove from the tile and paint the surfaces with alcohol ink. When the ink has dried, wet-sand both parts to remove ink from the high areas using a sanding sponge, accentuating the design and smoothing rough edges. Link the components using the smaller jumprings (see page 20). Hang from a chain or cord.

Earrings

YOU WILL NEED

Leftover clay from the main project

4 x matching color seed beads

2 x 10mm antique copper jumprings

2 x 1in (25mm) antique copper eyepins

2 x antique copper earwires

Chain-nose or flat-nose pliers

Use your leftover clay and follow the same steps for the pendant to create a similar pair of triangle shapes. Take an eyepin and thread on two seed beads. Make a simple loop at the end (see page 21). Attach the triangle to one end of the beaded pin and the earwire to the other end using chain- or flat-nose pliers. Open the loop on the beaded pin by twisting the loop to one side (do not pull it outward) and thread on the triangle. Close the loop by twisting it back until it lines up with the pin. Repeat this process to attach the earwire and complete the second earring the same way.

Try different arrangements for the clay strings. You don't need to stick to spirals or lines—try waves, wood grain patterns, and zigzags.

Arabian Nights

Well known for turquoise and gold colors, the Middle East has a rich color history. Sian Hamilton uses this as her starting point to design a set of jewelry pieces reminiscent of Arabian nights—using a textured stamp mat and a technique that gives a raised pattern finish.

FOR THE BRACELET YOU WILL NEED

1 block Premo! Sculpey Turquoise (5505)

½ block Premo! Sculpey Accents Antique Gold (5517)

Pasta machine

Texture stamp (by Lisa Pavelka)

Tissue blade or craft knife

20 x 1in (25mm) gold-colored eyepins

Round-nose pliers

1 x gold-colored magnetic clasp

12 x 6mm gold-colored jumprings

6 x 4mm gold-colored jumprings

Chain-nose pliers

Bracelet

1 Condition the Antique gold clay through the pasta machine at the thickest setting (see page 16). Use the Sutton slice technique to create a textured finish. To do this, take the texture mat and work with small pieces of clay. Push the clay firmly into the mat so that it fills the texture. Work on one small section at a time.

2 When you have about 1in (30mm) completed, take a flexible tissue blade and hold flat against the texture mat at one end of the blade. Pull the other end up to curve the blade and, keeping the end still against the mat, pivot the other end, pulling the blade across the mat, to take off layers of clay. Keep sliding the blade across the clay to reveal the texture.

3 Keep going with the Antique Gold clay until you have filled the texture mat. Roll a sheet of Turquoise clay through the pasta machine at setting No.1. Make sure the sheet covers the whole of the texture mat. Press the sheet down firmly making sure it is pressed down across the whole sheet.

4 Turn the mat over so the clay is flat against a non-stick surface. Gently pull the mat back as close to the clay as possible so the mat is almost bent double. Work very slowly. Stop if the clay pulls away with the mat and press down on that section again.

5 Revealing the texture requires patience so don't rush this or it will not work well. You really do need the Gold to come away with the Turquoise in one go, as it is really difficult to fix afterwards.

6 Lay the sheet on a surface you can cut on. Using the straight edge of a tissue blade, cut out five equal-sized rectangles. Use the pattern to guide you and cut out along the lines of the pattern with two repeats showing in each panel.

7 Take the eyepins and bend the wire into a zigzag shape so that it holds inside the panels without the need for glue. Use four for each panel piece, placing at the corners of each panel on the reverse side to the texture. Follow the image so that the loops sit right at the edge of the panels.

8 Roll another sheet of Turquoise through the pasta machine at setting No.1. Cut out five plain panels the same size as the textured ones. Back each textured panel with a plain piece, trapping the loop-ended wires in between the pieces. Press firmly together.

9 Bake the panel according to the manufacturer's instructions. Allow the clay to cool. Link all the panels together with 6mm jumprings (see page 20). Attach a clasp with the 4mm jumprings, using three on each side.

Earrings

YOU WILL NEED

Leftover Sutton slice sheet from the main project

2 x 8mm gold-colored jumprings

2 x gold-colored earwires

Ready-made gold-colored chain

Use small leftover pieces cut into a pleasing shape using a tissue blade. Make a hole in one end for a jumpring before baking, then bake, cool, and attach to earwires using jumprings (see page 20).

Pendant

YOU WILL NEED

Leftover Sutton slice sheet from the main project

⅝in (15mm) circle cutter

Needle tool

3 x 8mm gold-colored jumprings

Ready-made gold-colored chain

Put the leftover pieces of Sutton slice sheet through a pasta machine at setting No.1 to flatten the texture then cut out three pieces with a ⅝in (15mm) circle cutter. Make holes on both sides of the circles for jumprings, apart from the one that hangs at the bottom, using a needle tool. Bake, and when cool attach all the circles together with the jumprings (see page 20) and hang on a chain.

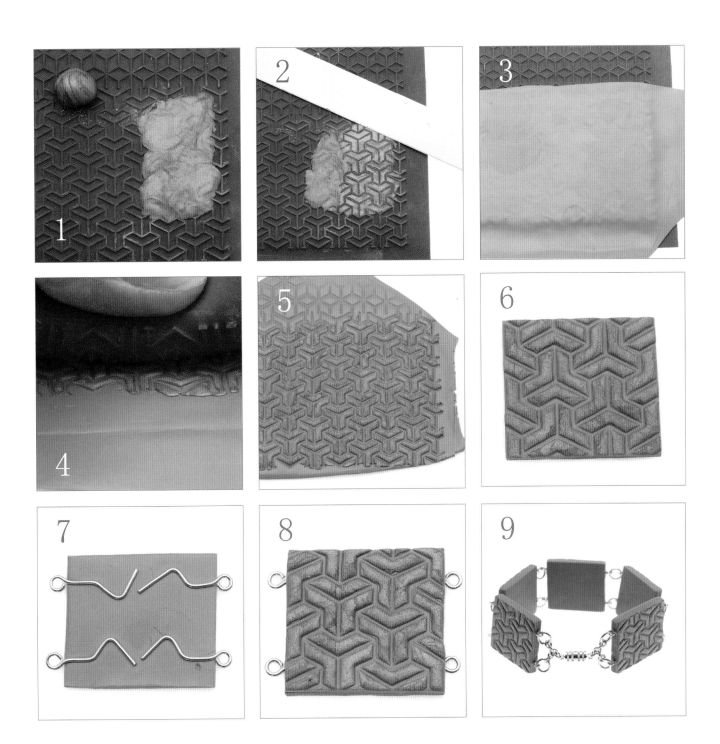

Mixed Media

*Alison Gallant combines cool blue-green pearl
and sizzling red to create a necklace and earrings
for hot, sunny, summer days.*

FOR THE NECKLACE YOU WILL NEED

1 block Premo! Sculpey Peacock Pearl (5038)

1 block Premo! Sculpey Pomegranate (5026)

½ block Premo! Sculpey White (5001)

¼ block Premo! Sculpey Black (5042)

Equivalent of 1 block scrap clay

Pasta machine

Cutters in 1¾in (43mm) and ¾in (18mm)

Tissue blade or craft knife

Needle tool

Fine-grit wet/dry sandpaper

20ft (6m) 1mm silver-colored copper wire

Flat-nose pliers and wire cutters

Polyester batting

Coarse cloth such as denim

Roll of nylon-coated beading wire

2 x 6mm jumprings

2 x crimp beads

1 x clasp

Necklace

1 Roll ½ block of Peacock Pearl through the pasta machine at setting No.1 (see page 16). Cut off a 2in (50mm) square piece. Slice strips about ⅛in (2mm) wide from the remainder. Twist each strip and lay randomly on the square sheet. Roll gently and pass through the pasta machine once. Turn 90 degrees, reduce the setting by one and roll through again. Put the piece on top of the remaining sheet. Using the same Peacock Pearl sheet, cut out the pendant shape. Take the larger cutter and cut a disc, then with the smaller disc cut a circle from of the middle but don't make it central; place the cutter off to one side so that you have one side thicker than the other.

2 Take ⅛ block of Pomegranate and roll into a log ⅝in (15mm) diameter. Roll ⅛ block of White through the pasta machine at setting No.2, ⅛ block Black at No.3, and ¼ block of Peacock Pearl at No.2. Wrap half the White around the Pomegranate. Trim the sides and roll to close the seam. Repeat with Black, White, and Peacock Pearl. Reduce to around ¼in (7mm) diameter by gently rolling.

3 Roll six beads around ⅝in (15mm) diameter from scrap clay. Cut thin slices from the cane and place around the scrap beads. Press together gently to close the seams and hide the scrap base then roll in your hands to reform into balls. Pierce each bead with the needle tool.

4 Roll sheets of Peacock Pearl, Pomegranate, Black, and 2 x White, in a variety of thicknesses from 1–3 on the pasta machine. Trim each to 1⅜ x 1¾in (35 x 45mm) and layer, pressing to exclude air between each one. Cut in half and stack. Trim one short end to straighten.

5 Roll ⅛ block of Peacock Pearl and Pomegranate into three logs each around ¼in (7mm) diameter and ¾in (18mm) long. Cut slices around 3/16in (5mm) thick from the colored stack. Lengthen the stripes by rolling through the pasta machine at setting No.1, then the next setting, and place around the log, trimming the length. Ease in extra stripes to fit. Roll gently to join the seams. Pierce with a needle tool through the barrel length.

6 From the remainder of the Peacock Pearl and Pomegranate, roll 10 balls in each color around ⅜in (10mm) in diameter. Flatten slightly and texture all sides with coarse sandpaper. Pierce the beads with the needle tool.

7 Take 30in (750mm) of wire. Hold one end with the flat-nose pliers and roll up the core of the bead quite tightly: three or four circles will do. Now roll with your fingers and keep randomly changing direction; ⅝in (15mm) from the end of the wire bend it by 90 degrees and, using your pliers, tuck in the end so that it doesn't show. Make another five beads.

8 Suspend all the beads on wire or place on polyester batting to bake according to the clay manufacturer's instructions. When the beads are cool, sand the focal, caned, and tube beads with sandpaper. Buff to a shine using coarse cloth or denim.

9 Cut 36in (900mm) of wire. Starting about 8in (200mm) along the wire, pass the short end through the hole in the pendant five times. Keep each coil close to the last. Randomly roll up the remaining wire on top of the focal bead, and tuck the ends in. Take the roll of beading wire and thread on all the beads, making sure the pendant goes in the center. Check you are happy with the length, then thread on a crimp bead and clasp. Bring the wire back through the crimp, and pull to make a small loop. Squeeze the crimp closed with pliers and repeat for the other side with a jumpring.

Place plastic wrap over the pendant before cutting out to provide smooth, rounded edges.

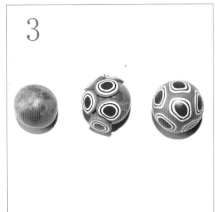

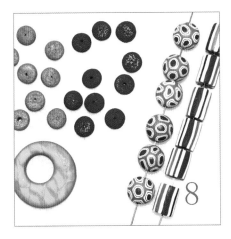

Earrings

YOU WILL NEED

Leftover clay from the main project

2 x 2in (50mm) silver-colored headpins

2 x silver-colored earwires

Chain or flat-nose pliers

Make two additional caned beads (as in Step 3), and two Pomegranate beads (as in Step 6), leaving them round and textured. Thread onto headpins and make a simple loop at the top (see page 21). Attach to earwires using chain- or flat-nose pliers. Open the loop on the earwire by twisting the loop to one side (do not pull it outward) and thread on the headpin. Close the loop by twisting it back in line with the earwire.

Protect your eyes and take great care when working with lengths of springy wire, as the ends are very sharp.

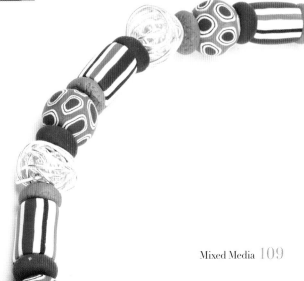

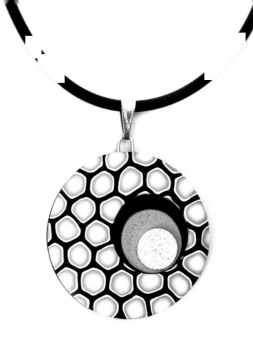

Lovely Layers

This striking set with a silver accent on each piece has been created by Alison Gallant. The designs include layers of textured polymer, which are accented by a patterned disc of silver metal clay.

FOR THE PENDANT YOU WILL NEED

½ block Premo! Sculpey Turquoise (5505)

½ block Premo! Sculpey White (5001)

½ block Premo! Sculpey Black (5042)

Pasta machine

Board or tile to work on

Paper

Tissue blade or craft knife

Texture sponge

Circle cutters in four sizes between ½–1¹³⁄₁₆in (12–45mm)

Plastic wrap

Domed surface

Wet/dry sandpaper

Teflon mat

Liquid polymer clay

1 x 12mm silver-colored disc with texture

Two-part epoxy resin

20mm silver-colored wire

Round-nose pliers

1 x silver-colored bail

Ready-made leather cord necklace

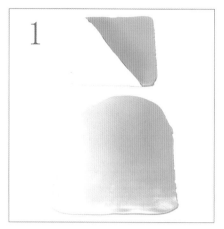

1

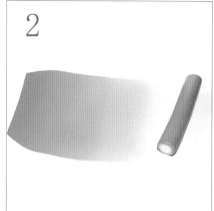

2

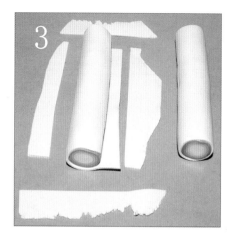

3

7

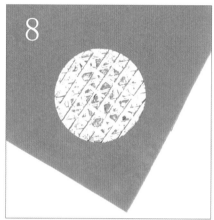

8

9

Trim light-colored or white ends of Skinner blend sheets to keep the centers of the canes clean.

Earrings

YOU WILL NEED

Leftover clay from the main project in Black and Turquoise

Cyanoacrylate adhesive (superglue)

2 x 12mm silver-colored discs

2 x silver-colored earwires

2 x 6mm silver-colored jumprings

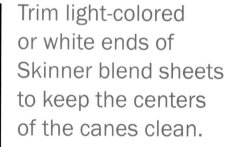

Stamp out two $^{13}/_{16}$in (20mm) discs in Black polymer clay and two of $^{5}/_{8}$in (16mm) in Turquoise. Make a small hole in each Black disc close to the edge. Bake, cool, and stick the Turquoise discs on top of the Black. Find the hole in the Black disc and place that at the top. Now line up the Turquoise disc with the Black at the bottom and glue together with superglue. Glue the silver discs to the front of the clay discs, placing them offcenter toward the bottom. Attach earwires using the jumprings (see page 20).

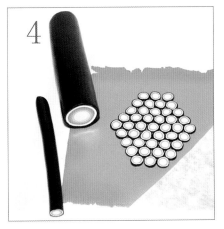

Pendant

1. Take a ¼ block each of Turquoise and White. To create an offset Skinner blend (see page 19), roll through the pasta machine at setting No.1 (see page 16). Fold from the bottom to the top and repeat until the colors are blended across the sheet, with a band of Turquoise on one side and White on the other.

2. Turn the blend 90 degrees. Roll through the pasta machine three times (the Turquoise edge entering first), reducing the thickness each time. Roll up tightly from White to Turquoise, making sure you don't trap any air. Rock the log back and forth to seal the seam.

3. Roll a ¼ block of White on setting No.4. Lay the log on the sheet and trim the White either end and along one long edge. Roll the log until the cut edge meets the remainder of the sheet. An indent will be formed and you can cut along the mark. Roll the log again to seal the seam.

4. Repeat using a ¼ block of Black rolled out at setting No.3. Reduce the log until the diameter is about ³⁄₁₆in (5mm). Roll ⅛ of a block of Turquoise at setting No.5 and place on the paper. Cut thin slices from the log and place close together on the sheet. Cover with paper and roll in every direction until there are no gaps.

5. Place plastic wrap over the sheet and stamp out a 1¹¹⁄₁₆in (43mm) circle. Remove the cling film. Carefully lift the circle with a blade and place on a domed surface. Stamp out an offset ¹³⁄₁₆in (20mm) circle and leave it in place. Bake, cool, and remove from the dome.

6. Roll out a ¼ block of Black on setting No.1 of the pasta machine. Texture and stamp out a 1¹¹⁄₁₆in (43mm) circle. Roll the trimmings on setting No.4, texture, and stamp out a 1³⁄₁₆in (30mm) circle. Bend a ¾in (20mm) length of silver-colored wire over round-nose pliers to make a "U" shape. Press under the edge of the larger circle. Stamp out a ⅝in (14mm) Turquoise circle, rolled through No.4. Bake all three according to the clay manufacturer's instructions.

7. Sand the base of the domed piece with fine sandpaper. Stick the "U" shape to the clay with two-part epoxy resin glue and the ¹³⁄₁₆in (20mm) circle to the plain side of the larger one, offcenter, with liquid polymer clay. Smear a small amount on the flat surface of the dome and press firmly to the base. Bake.

8. Take the silver-colored disc and sand the back to roughen up the surface to help the glue stick.

9. Take a silver piece and stick onto the ⁹⁄₁₆in (14mm) Turquoise circle, offset, and then stick it inside the pendant window. Attach a bail and string as desired.

Bangle

YOU WILL NEED

Leftover cane from the main project

Black polymer clay

1 x channel bangle blank

Roll out a sheet of Black polymer clay through the pasta machine at setting No.1. Cut slices of cane and press into the Black clay in a row. Trim with a tissue blade and insert into the channel of the bangle. Smooth the clay gently with the side of your finger to avoid fingerprints. Bake and sand when cool.

Love & Lace

Sue Corrie takes inspiration from pretty scraps of fabric and creates a romantic set of jewelry pieces from lace.

FOR THE COLLAR YOU WILL NEED

2 x blocks polymer clay (scrap clay mixed with black)

Length of lace to fit a collar

Craft roller

Tissue blade or craft knife

Bamboo skewer

Needle tool

Gold acrylic paint

Mica powder in Turquoise and Flamingo Pink

18in (45cm) of ⅛in (3mm) diameter rubber cord

Cookie tray

Polyester batting

Acrylic varnish

1 x decorative bail (with loop)

1 x large freshwater pearl

4 x large-holed spacer beads

2 x cord ends

1 x toggle clasp

2 x silver-colored jumprings

Cyanoacrylate adhesive (superglue)

1 x 2in (50mm) silver-colored headpin

Earrings

YOU WILL NEED

Leftover clay from main project

Polymer clay in a contrasting color

2 x 1in (25mm) silver-colored headpins

2 x 4mm silver-colored patterned beads

2 x silver-colored earwires

Roll out a sheet of clay as in Step 1 of the main project and back the clay with another contrasting color sheet before imprinting with fine lace. Cut 3¼ x ³⁄₁₆in (80 x 5mm) strips and curl round a skewer. Remove and pinch one end closed. Push a headpin through the pinched end from inside before baking. Add a bead to the headpins and make a simple loop (see page 21). Attach to earwires using chain- or flat-nose pliers. Open the loop on the earwire by twisting the loop to one side (do not pull it outward) and thread on the headpin. Close the loop by twisting it back in line with the earwire.

Collar

1 Condition all clay (see page 16). You'll need to make four beads in total for the collar. For each bead: roll out a ¹⁄₃₂in (1mm) sheet of polymer clay about 3½in (90mm) square. Dampen the lace and stretch it across the sheet below the center. Gently press it into the clay. Use your craft roller to help you embed the lace firmly. After removing the lace, run a blade under the clay sheet to free it from the work surface.

2 Roll out a ⅛in (3mm) sheet of clay about 3½ x 2½in (90 x 60mm). Wrap one long edge over a skewer to form a top channel for the bead. Smooth the join. Place the square sheet over it, so that the upper edge of the lace pattern falls near the top of the channel. Slowly smooth it into place, front and back. Take care not to trap air between the clay sheets.

3 Look at the lace pattern to decide where to trim the ends. Twist the skewer to loosen the bead. Slide each end partway off and cut neatly with a blade. Trim the bottom of the bead using a craft knife so that it follows the lace edge. Impress the bottom edge with the side of a needle tool to create a natural scalloped edge for the lace.

4 Take some gold acrylic paint on your finger. Dab the paint on raised parts of the design, a little at a time. Allow it to dry slightly between coats. Cover the edges—you may prefer to keep the back clean. Follow with the Mica powder. Build up the colors until you get an effect you like. You can use a fine brush to pick out small areas of pattern.

5 String the four beads on a piece of rubber cord to keep the channel open. Curve them with your fingers to form a nice collar shape. Make frills by shaping each bead over a skewer. Remove the cord. Bake the beads in the oven on a cookie sheet with a layer of polyester batting underneath for at least 40 minutes at the clay manufacturer's recommended temperature. Place extra pieces of batting under the frills to support them.

6 Once the beads are cool, seal them with acrylic varnish and buff to a shine with a soft cloth. String on to the rubber cord as follows: spacer, clay bead, spacer, clay bead, bail, clay bead, spacer, clay bead, spacer. Glue the cord ends on and attach a decorative toggle clasp to each end using jumprings (see page 20). Place the pearl bead on the headpin and make a simple loop above the bead (see page 21). Attach this loop to the decorative bail.

Ribbon charm

YOU WILL NEED

Leftover clay from main project

Polymer clay in a contrasting color

3 x 1in (25mm) silver-colored headpins

1 x 8mm silver-colored patterned beads

1 x 6mm silver-colored patterned beads

2 x 10mm silver-colored jumprings

1 x silver-colored eyepin

Ribbon

Use the instructions for making earrings to make up three spiral pieces on headpins. Attach all three pieces to one 10mm jumpring (see page 20). Take the eyepin and thread on the two metal beads. Make a simple loop at the end (see page 21). Attach this piece to the spirals and add another 10mm jumpring to the opposite end. Tie on an attractive ribbon, which you can then use to tie this decoration to a handbag or purse.

For a more delicate look, try stringing onto a $^1/_{32}$in (1mm) beading chain or tiger tail wire with a piece of silk ribbon at each end.

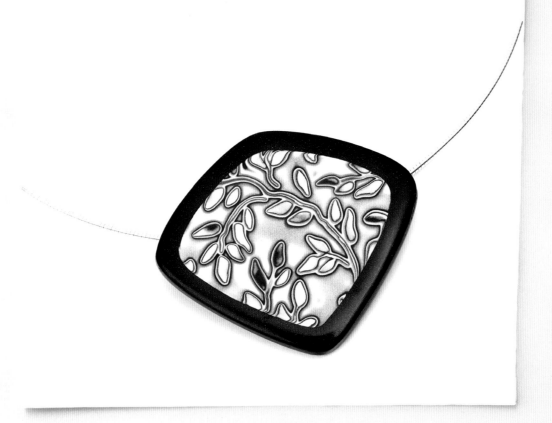

Coastal Collection

Patterns found in nature are the theme of this beautiful collection by Melanie Muir, inspired by the sea and the shoreline.

FOR THE PENDANT YOU WILL NEED

½ block Premo! Sculpey Black (5042)

½ block Premo! Sculpey Antique Gold (5517)

½ block Premo! Sculpey White (5001)

Pasta machine

Texture sheets/stamps

Tissue blade or craft knife

Sheet of blank copy paper

Parchment paper

Scalpel

Plastic shape template

Cyanoacrylate adhesive (superglue)

Wet/dry sandpaper

Pin vise and drill bit (optional)

Fine permanent marker pen

2 x small rubber O-rings

Drill bit (slightly larger than O-rings)

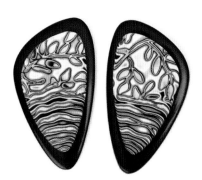

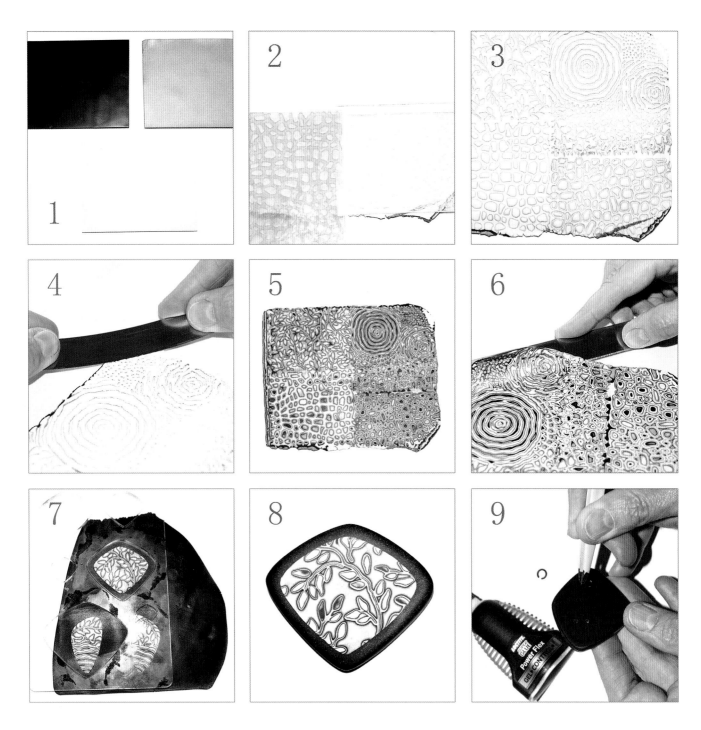

You can put polyester batting over the top of your pieces when baking to protect from burning or discoloring.

Necklace

1 Choose three colors, which are dark/medium/light in contrast, roll to No.3 setting (see page 16) on the pasta machine, then stack. Then roll through the pasta machine at No.1, then No.3, cut in half and stack again. Repeat. You should see the darkest color four times; cut off a strip to check.

2 Lightly spritz the clay with water to act as a resist. Use a texture stamp/sheet with a very deep etch (minimum ⅛in/2mm) to make a really clear impression. Use different textures to create variety.

3 Press down as hard as you can and work with your fingers or a hard block to get the best results. You will end up with mounds and dips of textured polymer.

4 Using a thin, flexible tissue blade, shave off the tops of the mounds down to the dips, holding your blade as shown and using a slight sideways sawing motion. Take a deep breath, go slow, and don't panic—if you cut too deep, simply stop and reverse out.

5 Smooth the veneer completely by rubbing hard with a smooth pebble or shiny card over the top of a sheet of copy paper. Peel back the paper to check progress if need be.

6 Slide a stiff tissue blade under the veneer at a 45-degree angle and keeping it firm to the tile base, slide back and forth while gently lifting to remove the veneer. Place it onto non-stick/parchment paper or similar. You will be able to make lots of things from one sheet of veneer!

7 Use a plastic shape template to identify an interesting area of pattern, then cut it out; it's easier if you lean your scalpel against the wall of the template. Cut the same size and shape out of a piece of plain clay in a complementary/contrasting color (rolled on setting No.3), place the veneer piece inside the "window" and smooth the joins using the copy paper technique again. Cut out the whole piece using the next size up on the template t creates a frame. To back, press onto another plain piece of clay, rolled to No.1. Smooth with layout paper technique. Cut out again. Place on card or paper and bake according to the clay manufacturer's instructions.

8 Sand and polish your pendant with water, using sandpaper to shape and smooth, then polish. For a satin finish, simply rub on a cloth. You can leave the reverse matt.

9 Measure and mark two points slightly up from the horizontal center, about 1in (25mm) apart, one about ³⁄₁₆in (5mm) below the other. Using a drill bit slightly larger than the O-rings, drill these holes carefully to a depth of no more than ⅛in (2mm). Using the superglue and a needle or similar, carefully place a small dot of glue in each of the four holes. Glue in first one end of each O-ring, then the other. Leave to set for a few minutes and pull to test the bond. Thread onto your chosen wire, ribbon, or cable.

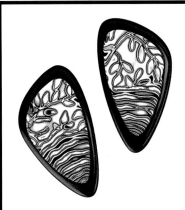

Earrings

YOU WILL NEED

Leftover clay from main project

2 x silver-colored ear posts with flat pads

Make matching earrings using the same cut and frame process, but make the backing much thinner (roll on pasta machine setting No.6). Glue ear posts onto the backs with a strong industrial glue or two-part epoxy resin.

Butterfly Heaven

These butterflies will brighten your day. Sian Hamilton shows you how well they can work in jewelry designs with this stunning trio of butterfly-themed designs.

FOR THE PENDANT YOU WILL NEED

Scrap clay in Premo! Sculpey Cadmium Yellow Hue (5572), Cadmium Red Hue (5382), Black (5042), and White (5001)

Pasta machine

Tissue blade or craft knife

Paintbrush or knitting needle

3 x 1in (25mm) eyepins

18in (45cm) fine-curb chain

1 x clasp

Premo! Sculpey gloss glaze

2 x 6mm jumprings

Teflon or non-stick sheet

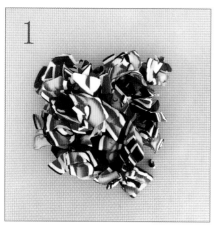

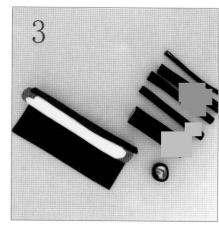

Pendant

1 Gather together your scrap clay and condition it by rolling it through setting No.1 on the pasta machine (see page 16). Working on a non-stick sheet (such as Teflon) chop up the mixture of clays into fine pieces with a tissue blade or craft knife.

2 Form the chopped-up clay into a roll. It needs to be about ¾in (18mm) wide. The length will be determined by how much clay you have; the width is more important. Cut a section off the roll to check how the colors are distributed. If you don't like what you see, then chop up again and roll it again.

3 To make canes take a small amount of Yellow and Red clay and mix together until streaky. Roll into a tube about ¼in (6mm) wide. Roll out a sheet of Black clay to setting No.4 on a pasta machine. Cover the Yellow/Red tube in a sheet. Cut the tube in half and reduce one piece to about ⅛in (2mm) across. Cut into sections the same length as the roll created in Step 2.

4 Form the roll from Step 2 into a teardrop shape and add canes from Step 3 to the wider end. Use five ⅛in (2mm) canes in a row, then cut one ⅛in (2mm) cane in half lengthwise and on top to fill in between. Push all the canes together until they start to look like one cane and you can't see between them.

5 Keep rolling the cane to make a teardrop shape with the smaller canes at the wider end. Take another piece of Black clay and make a sheet using setting No.2 on the pasta machine. Cover the teardrop in a sheet of Black, with the seam at the pointed end.

6 Cut the cane in half and leave one piece as a teardrop. Take the other piece and pinch the wider end into a point. This is to make the top wing of the butterfly; keep working on the cane until it is the shape you want. Place both canes in the refrigerator for a minimum of 30 minutes.

7 When the canes have become firmer, take them out of the refrigerator and, using a tissue blade, cut thin strips off both canes. The pieces should be about ⅛in (2–3mm) thick. You need two pieces of both canes.

8 Take the ¼in (6mm) cane from Step 3 and cut it in half lengthwise. Cut off a piece about ⅝in (15mm) long and round off both edges then roll to reduce to ⅛in (3mm) wide. This is the body of the butterfly so try and keep the Yellow/Red center in the middle.

9 Add the wing sections from Step 7 to the body. Push the wings gently into the body and then use the handle end of a paintbrush or knitting needle to roll all the sections together. Try not to spread the clay too far; you just want it all to stick together. Finally, cut an eye pin so it is slightly shorter than the body and push into the top. Bake according to the manufacturer's instructions. When cool, brush with a coat of gloss varnish. To make a necklace, take the two remaining eyepins and create loops at the straight ends (see page 21). Attach both eyepins to the loop at the top of the butterfly and attach the other ends to the chain (see page 20). Find the middle of the chain and open that link. Attach the clasp to one end and a jumpring to the other.

Use up scrap clay in any color to make the canes for this project. Always add a single-color sheet around the edge.

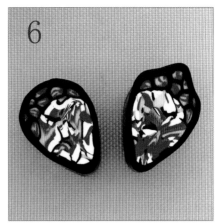

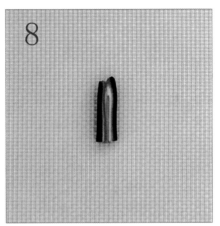

Earrings

YOU WILL NEED

Leftover cane from
main project

2 x 2in (50mm) lengths
of black fine curb chain

1in (25mm) piece of
black wire

2 x black-colored earwires

Reduce the canes (see page 17) to make mini
butterflies. At Step 6, cut the cane into more pieces
and reduce a couple to about ¼in (6mm) to make tiny
butterflies. Reduce the canes before you refrigerate, as
cold canes will not reduce easily. Follow the main project
steps to make the butterflies. Hang from fine chain by
opening the last link on the chain using two pairs of
pliers; this can be fiddly so be patient (see page 20).
Add earwires to the tops of the chain in the same way.

Brooch

YOU WILL NEED

Left over cane from main project

1 x brooch bar

Two-part epoxy resin

Follow the main steps of the project but instead of putting
one eyepin in the body (at Step 9) place two side-by-
side as eyes and bake following the clay manufacturer's
instructions. Lastly, glue on a brooch bar using two-part
epoxy resin or thick gel.

Love Bears

Lynn Allingham's cute embellished set of love bears on a kilt pin with matching necklace will bring a light-hearted, sweet touch to any outfit.

FOR THE KILT PIN YOU WILL NEED

1 x block Fimo Sahara

1 x block Fimo Caramel

Scrap of Fimo Black, for the eyes

2 x antique gold headpins

Scrap paper for baking

Bottle of clear liquid varnish

3 x miniature wooden half spools

Brown embroidery thread

Two-part epoxy resin

6in (15cm) of ⅜in (9mm) red gingham ribbon

1 x antique gold kilt pin

4.8mm antique gold x curb chain

2mm antique gold trace chain

Wire cutters

6 x small red heart buttons

1 x gold puffy heart charm

8 x 7mm antique gold jumprings

3 x 5mm antique gold jumprings

Round-nose and flat-nose pliers

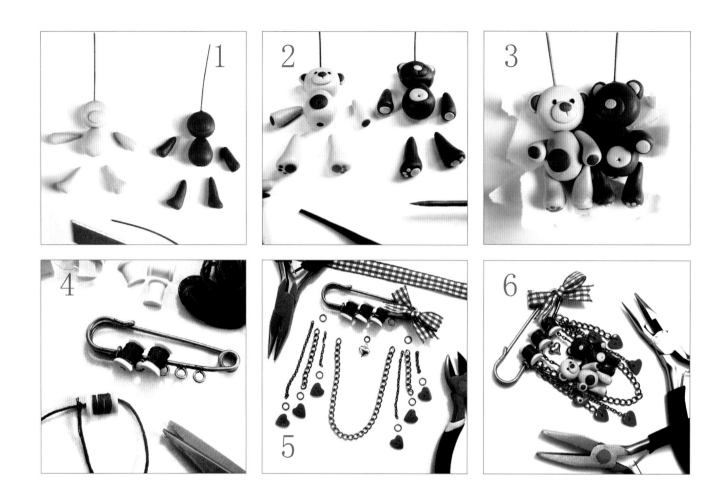

When using polymer clay, try to handle the clay as little as possible and keep it cool.

Use tiny paper wedges to keep the bears' arms and legs in position while baking.

Kilt Pin

1 Take both the Sahara and Caramel clay and form into basic bear body shapes by warming and sculpting the clay between your fingers. Make a head, body, arms, and legs. Insert a headpin from the bottom through the body and head, being careful not to distort the shape.

2 Take the Sahara and Caramel clay again, but this time use them in contrast to create the small detail. Add paws, chest, nose, and eye detail by rolling small balls of clay and gently patting them flat and into place using your fingertips. Make ears by creating two contrasting flat circles and cut in half. Gently place onto the head.

3 Handle the clay very gently and slowly move your bears into position. Once you are happy with their shape, use small, folded pieces of paper to keep any limbs propped up during baking. Bake according to the manufacturer's instructions. Leave to cool, varnish, then bake again. Once the clay is cool and hardened, snip and loop the headpin (see page 21).

4 Take a mini wooden spool and tie a generous length of brown embroidery thread onto it. Wind the thread several times around the spool and tie tightly at the back. Add spools onto the kilt pin by tying thoroughly into position. Once all three are tied, add a small amount of glue to the back to fix them.

5 Tie a generous length of 9mm red gingham ribbon onto the end of the kilt pin, tie into a neat bow and trim. Cut a total of six pieces of both fine and chunky chain as desired and add buttons using jumprings (see page 20). Cut a length of chunky chain that will droop beneath the bears from the first and fifth loop.

6 Attach all chains to loops one and five using jumprings. Attach one gold puffy heart to the third loop using a jumpring. Attach the bears from both heads, add a few links of chain to make sure they hang in the desired position then attach with jumprings to the remaining loops.

Necklace

YOU WILL NEED

Fimo clay as in the main project steps

1 x small red heart button

1 x antique gold headpin

Ready-made antique gold chain

1 x 5mm antique gold jumpring

Make a little bear necklace by repeating Steps 1–3. Once baked and varnished, glue a small red button heart into place on his chest with a strong industrial glue or two-part epoxy resin. Hang him from a ready-made chain using a jumpring (see page 20) attached to the loop in his head.

Teatime Treats

Lynn Allingham shows you how to create and wear this fun and fanciful set of decadent afternoon tea treats.

FOR THE NECKLACE YOU WILL NEED

1 x block Fimo Cognac

1 x block Fimo White

1 x block Fimo Transparent Yellow

Needle tool

Tissue blade or craft knife

Star nib

Silicone cream clay in White, Pink, and Brown

Fine iridescent glitter

1 x miniature two-tier cake stand

Deco sauce in pink and brown

Metal glue

Silver-colored trace chain

1 x ribbon bow

6 x 3mm red glass beads

2 x white rocaille beads

3 x jumprings

1 x trigger clasp

Pliers

Wire cutters

Ring

YOU WILL NEED

Fimo clay as in the main project steps

Dolls' house miniature ceramic plate and fork

Silicone cream clay in White

Craft metal glue

3 x miniature fruit canes

1 x ring blank

To make your slice of pie, roll out Cognac clay through setting No.1 on the pasta machine (see page 16). Roll out Transparent Yellow clay to the same thickness, place two layers together and then add to the on top of the cognac. Repeat again using the White clay and place on top of the Yellow. Slice into a wedge shape with a blade. Add a piece of Cognac sheet to the back of the pie wedge to make the pie edge. Bake, then decorate the same way as the main step instructions, then bake again. Glue to a miniature plate with a craft metal glue and add a couple of fruit slices on the side and a fork. When the glue is dry, glue the whole thing to a flat pad ring blank.

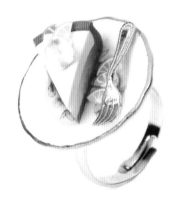

Necklace

1 Take a marble-sized amount of Cognac clay and roll out. Make indentations along the outer edge with a needle tool. Using a craft knife, lightly score the clay creating diamond shapes. Cut into wafers ⅜in (9mm) thick. Take a new piece of clay and roll then cut it into small sections. Roll into a ball and flatten. Use a rounded implement to create a cup shape. Dent around the edges. Make six of these then bake.

2 Fix four cases to a firm surface using double-sided tape to avoid any movement. Apply the small star nib to the White cream clay. Pipe in small circular motions to create cream topping; make two of these in White. Next, use the star nib on the Pink cream clay and pipe as before; this will create two pink cupcakes with white edges.

3 Place the star nib straight onto the Brown cream clay and squeeze a little excess out until you see the brown coming through. Take another two cases and pipe as before to create chocolate cupcakes with a white edge.

4 Gather together all the items needed for decorating; this needs to be done quickly while the cream clay is still nice and wet. Sprinkle with fine iridescent glitter as desired and add red glass beads to the tops of every cupcake. Add Deco sauce as required, squeezing slowly and gently. Lastly, add wafers and fruit slices, then leave for 24 hours to fully dry and fix (no baking needed).

5 You now have six cupcakes. You only need five but it is always a good idea to make a spare in case anything goes wrong. Take the two-tier cake stand and glue two cupcakes onto the top tier and three onto the lowest tier as desired. Decorate the base by adding fruit slices in between the cakes.

6 Measure and cut silver trace chain to the desired length. Add a trigger clasp with a jumpring (see page 20) to one end and a single jumpring to the other. Carefully cut the chain on one side and add a pink bow using a jumpring and two white beads. Thread on your tiered cupcake pendant and your necklace is complete.

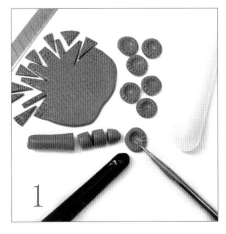

1

2

To create a hole in polymer clay, push a headpin through the piece, bake, and remove to leave a neat hole.

3

4

5

6

When using silicone cream clay, always let it dry before removing from the nibs.

Summer Picnic

This picnic-inspired brooch and ring by Lynn Allingham is a reminder of hot, lazy summer days and delicious outdoor food.

FOR THE BROOCH YOU WILL NEED

Small amounts of Fimo in colors: Sahara, Cognac, Brown, Light Green, Dark Green, Pink, White, Red, and Yellow

Old toothbrush

Tissue blade or craft knife

Craft roller

Miniature cup, saucer, spoon, and cup for saucepot

Miniature wooden woven basket

Red gingham material

Metal glue

Scissors

Brown and red Deco sauce

Fruit clay canes

4¾in (120mm) x 2mm gold trace chain

Small color-coordinating beads

2 x 4mm gold-colored jumprings

2 x gold-colored eye pins

2 x gold- or silver-colored brooch bars

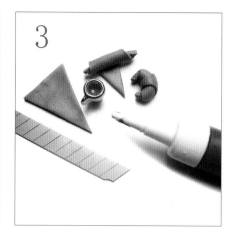

If clay is stiff, cup it in the palm of your hands, breathe on it, and roll the clay to heat it up and soften it.

Ring

Polymer clay in Cognac

Miniature cup, saucer, and spoon

Small square of red gingham material

Brown Deco sauce

1 x fruit clay cane

1 x gold-colored ring blank with flat pad

Cut a square of red gingham to line the saucer and glue on with a craft metal glue. Place a miniature cup on top, fill it with brown Deco sauce, and embellish as desired following the steps of the main project. Make another croissant following Step 3 of the main project. When all the pieces needing baking are cool, glue together with a craft metal glue. Finish by adding a miniature spoon and glue onto a gold ring blank.

Brooch

1 Take the Sahara clay and roll it out thinly; slice one side off straight. Roll out a strip of Brown clay, again slicing one side straight, and lay the cut edges flush together. Trim the Brown off to create a crust. Stipple the surface with a toothbrush to create a bread texture then cut it into triangular sandwich shapes.

2 Mix two Greens to make lettuce and roll out very thinly and about ⅝in (15mm) in diameter. Repeat as before using White and Pink clay to create ham. Take the Red clay and roll it into a cylindrical shape; chop up to make tomatoes. Take the Yellow clay, roll out very thinly, and shape. Carefully assemble your sandwich: bread, tomatoes, lettuce, cheese, ham, and bread.

3 Roll out some Cognac clay quite thinly and cut into a long triangular shape. Tightly roll from the larger end down to the point then slightly bend each side inward to create a croissant shape. Bake according to the manufacturer's instructions. While they are baking, take a tiny miniature cup and fill with red Deco sauce. Leave to dry.

4 Cut a piece of red gingham material. Gently fray the edges for a rustic look. Glue the material into the miniature basket as desired. Once the glue is dry, assemble the sandwiches, croissant, and saucepot as desired and fix into place.

5 Now you need to assemble the second part of the double brooch. Take a miniature cup, saucer, and spoon, and then glue them together. Add brown Deco sauce to the cup or tea and embellish as desired with clay cane fruit pieces.

6 Take a length of gold trace chain. On each end of the chain, assemble two color-coordinating beads using eyepins. Use 4mm jumprings to attach one end of the chain to the basket handle and the other to the cup handle (see page 20). To complete the design, simply glue brooch bars to the back of both pieces.

A coat of liquid polymer clay will hold your item together and make it more durable when baked.

Sail Away

This cute sailing-boat themed set is by Sian Hamilton. The layering of polymer clay works perfectly to create the effect of ocean waves.

FOR THE PENDANT YOU WILL NEED

½ block Premo! Sculpey Ultramarine Blue (5092)

½ block Premo! Sculpey White (5001)

½ block Premo! Sculpey Cadmium Red Hue (5382)

Pasta machine

Tissue blade or craft knife

Craft roller

1 x pendant blank

Knitting needle

Ready-made silver-colored trace chain

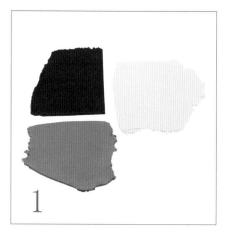

Pendant

1 Take 1in (25mm) pieces of both Ultramarine Blue and White clay and condition well until they are soft and pliable (see page 16). Create the medium blue color by mixing half the Ultramarine and half the White together. Roll all three colors into sheets at setting No.4 on the pasta machine.

2 Using a tissue blade or craft knife, cut all the pieces into long strips about ¼in (6mm) wide. Stack them together, placing them randomly so that you don't get an even stripe. The colored stripes can be wider toward the base.

3 Once you have a stack that is about 1¼in (32mm) high, squash it to bond all the pieces and cut it in half widthwise, then stack the two pieces together. You don't want the two pieces to line up completely, as the mismatched pieces will add to the effect.

4 Work the block by squashing it, then rolling it out a bit with a craft roller, but not too far; you want the colors to start to move about but still stay in stripes. When you think you've done enough, stand the block up and cut down into slices about ⅛in (2–3mm) thick.

5 Using the pendant blank for guidance, cut down one of the slices from Step 4 to fit into the frame; the piece needs to be about ⅛in (2mm) thick. You are looking for a piece that has some color movement at the top to look like waves. Cut the pieces so that you have two sections that fill about two-thirds of the pendant.

6 To make the boat, condition and roll out small pieces of White and Cadmium Red clays through the pasta machine at setting No.2. The white strip needs to be about ½in (13mm) wide and the red strip should be ³⁄₁₆in (4mm) wide. Cut two long triangles for the sails with one longer than the other and a slanted shape for the boat.

7 Put the boat pieces to one side. Go back to the sea sections and add a tapered white slice and medium blue slice to fill the pendant blank. Roll sheets of clay at setting No.2 on the pasta machine and use the pendant blank to get the size right. Keep the sections separate at the moment.

8 Take the bottom piece from Step 5 and back it with a very thin sheet of clay (the color doesn't matter). It should be a little higher than the other section in the frame to make the boat look like it is sitting in the water. Place all the pieces of the background into the frame and push them together until you can't see the separate pieces.

9 Place the hull of the boat up against the bottom sea section and using a knitting needle smooth the boat into the sea. You want to create a small curve in the blue clay so that the boat looks like it's floating. Smooth out the clay either side of the boat level with the frame at the sides. Add the sails above the boat. Clean up the frame edges with a knife and make sure all the clay is smooth and fingerprint-free. Bake according to the clay manufacturer's instructions. Cool and add a chain.

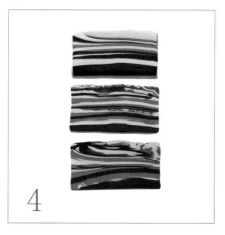

4

5

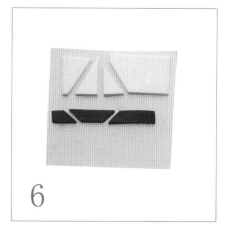

6

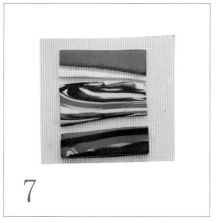

7

8

9

Necklace

YOU WILL NEED

Leftover clay from
main project

1 x 2in (50mm)
silver-colored headpin

Ready-made silver-colored
fine curb chain

Make a larger boat shape for a pendant following
Step 6 of the main project and add a thin strip of red
in between the white sails. This boat is approx. 1in
(25mm) tall from the tip of the sails to the base of the
red hull. Make a curl of blue and white clay as a swirl
underneath, using any scrap clay left over from the main
project. Before baking, push a long headpin from the
bottom of the boat to the top and then add the blue sea
curl underneath so the headpin is enclosed between
the boat and sea clay. Bake the clay. Make a simple loop
at the top of the headpin (see page 21). Make the loop
quite large and thread onto a fine ready-made chain.

Earrings

YOU WILL NEED

Leftover clay from
main project

2 x 1in (25mm) silver-colored headpins

2 x silver-colored earwires

Make two small boats ⅜in (10mm) tall using clay
sheets rolled through the pasta machine at setting
No.1. Following Step 6 of the main project instructions,
cut the white sails evenly and add a thin strip of red
between the sails. Push a headpin from the base
through the middle so it extends centrally out of the
top. Bake and create simple loops (see page 21) above
the boats. Attach to earwires using chain- or flat-nose
pliers. Open the loop (see page 20) on the earwire by
twisting the loop to one side (do not pull it outward)
and thread on the headpin. Close the loop by twisting
it back in line with the earwire.

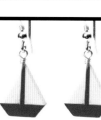

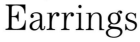

Resources

UK

Bead Aura
3 Neal's Yard
Covent Garden
London
WC2H 9DP
Tel: +44 (0)20 7836 3002
www.beadaura.co.uk

Beads Direct Ltd
10 Duke Street
Loughborough
Leicestershire
LE11 1ED
Tel: +44 (0)1509 218028
www.beadsdirect.co.uk

The Bead Merchant
PO Box 5025
Coggeshall
Essex
CO6 1HW
Tel: +44 (0)1376 570022
www.beadmerchant.co.uk

The Bead Shop
44 Higher Ardwick
Manchester
M12 6DA
Tel: +44 (0)161 274 4040
www.the-beadshop.co.uk

Beadsisters
Mid Cairngarroch Croft
Stoneykirk
Stranraer
Wigtownshire
DG9 9EH
Tel: +44 (0)1776 830352
www.beadsisters.co.uk

Beadtime
Beadtime Warehouse
Unit 16, Shepperton Business
Park
Govett Avenue
Shepperton
TW17 8BA
Tel: +44 (0)1932 244700
www.beadtime.co.uk

ClayAround
Larkrise
Garthmyl
Montgomery
Powys
SY15 6SB
Tel: +44 (0)1686 640745
www.clayaround.com

Craft Cellar
10 Towthorpe Road
Haxby
York
YO32 3ND
Tel: +44 (0)113 8150050
www.craftcellar.co.uk

**The Genuine Gemstone
Company Limited**
Unit 2D Eagle Road
Moons Moat
Redditch
Worcestershire
B98 9HF
Tel: +44 (0)800 6444 655
www.jewellerymaker.com

Palmer Metals Ltd
401 Broad Lane
Coventry
CV5 7AY
Tel: +44 (0)845 644 9343
www.palmermetals.co.uk

Spoilt Rotten Beads
7 The Green
Haddenham
Ely
Cambridgeshire
CB6 3TA
Tel: +44 (0)1353 749853
www.spoiltrottenbeads.co.uk

Shiney Rocks
14 Sandy Park Road,
Brislington
Bristol
BS4 3PE
Tel: +44 (0)117 300 9800
www.shineyrocks.co.uk

USA

Beadin' Path
15 U.S. 1
Freeport
ME 04032
Tel: +1 207-650-1557
www.beadinpath.com

**Fire Mountain Gems
and Beads**
1 Fire Mountain Way
Grants Pass
OR 97526-2373
Tel: +1 800-355-2137
(toll free)
Tel: +1 541-956-7890
www.firemountaingems.com

PolymerClay Express
105 West Main Street
New Market
MD 21774
Tel: +1 800 844 7260
(toll free)
Tel: +1 301 882 7260
www.polymerclayexpress.com

Polymer Clay Superstore
6861 Penn Avenue
Wernersville
PA 19565
Tel: +1 610 693 4039
www.polymerclaysuperstore.
com

**Vintaj Natural Brass
Company**
PO box 246
Galena, Il 61036
www.vintaj.com

Index

To place an order, or to request a catalog, contact:
GMC Publications Ltd
Castle Place, 166 High Street, Lewes, East Sussex, BN7 1XU
United Kingdom
Tel: +44 (0)1273 488005
Website: www.gmcbooks.com